W9-DIW-721

DATE DUE

SEP 1 5 1983		
JAN 0 3 199		

HIGHSMITH 45-220

ROOTS OF DETECTION

RECOGNITIONS

detective/suspense
Bruce Cassiday, General Editor

Raymond Chandler by Jerry Speir
P. D. James by Norma Siebenheller
John D. MacDonald by David Geherin
Ross Macdonald by Jerry Speir
The Murder Mystique: Crime Writers on Their Art
edited by Lucy Freeman
Dorothy L. Sayers by Dawson Gaillard
Sons of Sam Spade: The Private Eye Novel in the 70s
by David Geherin

science fiction/fantasy
Sharon Jarvis, General Editor

Isaac Asimov by Jean Fiedler and Jim Mele
Ray Bradbury by Wayne L. Johnson
Critical Encounters: Writers and Themes in Science Fiction
edited by Dick Riley
Critical Encounters II: Writers and Themes in Science Fiction
edited by Tom Staicar
The Feminine Eye: Science Fiction and the Women Who Write It
edited by Tom Staicar
Frank Herbert by Timothy O'Reilly
Ursula K. LeGuin by Barbara J. Bucknall
Theodore Sturgeon by Lucy Menger

Also of Interest
The Bedside, Bathtub & Armchair Companion to Agatha Christie
edited by Dick Riley and Pam McAllister
Introduction by Julian Symons

ROOTS OF DETECTION

The Art of Deduction
before Sherlock Holmes

Edited by
Bruce Cassiday

FREDERICK UNGAR PUBLISHING CO.
NEW YORK

Library of Congress Cataloging in Publication Data
Main entry under title:

Roots of detection.

(Recognitions)
1. Detective and mystery stories.   I. Cassiday,
Bruce.   II. Series.
PN6120.95.D45R6   1983   808.83′872   83-3571
ISBN 0-8044-2113-7
ISBN 0-8044-6065-5 (pbk.)

Contents

ROOTS OF DETECTION

Deduction in Literature before Sherlock Holmes

AN INTRODUCTION

Long before Sherlock Holmes came onto the literary scene with his famous explanation of the art of deduction in *A Study in Scarlet*, classic literature had produced isolated gems of intuitive reasoning, strewing them amidst the fables, myths, and legends that make up humanity's reservoir of written knowledge.

Yet many fans of detective fiction think of Holmes as the inventor, in 1887, of the art of deduction when he says to his new friend, Dr. Watson, "You have been in Afghanistan, I perceive." At the doctor's astonishment that Holmes knows what he has not been told, the detective explains the deductive process by telling *how* he knows.

"The train of thoughts ran so swiftly through my mind that I arrived at the conclusion without being conscious of intermediate steps," he says. "There were such steps, however." He outlines his observations: medical man with military air, hence, army doctor; face darkened by tropical exposure; haggard from sickness and injury. "Where in the tropics could an English army doctor have seen such hardship and get his arm wounded? Clearly in Afghanistan."

Holmes's deduction—that, since Watson is an army doctor who has seen action, he has obviously been in Afghanistan—is an inferential surmise based on observed evidence and consciously known facts.

The actual deduction, or inference, is in the form of a syllogism that takes place in Holmes's mind as he makes this lightning connection. He combines a major and a minor premise—*major premise*; that Watson, from his appearance, has been serving in the military; *minor premise*: that the British armed forces have been fighting in Afghanistan—and comes to a conclusion: that Watson has been in Afghanistan.

The art of deduction, as exemplified here, is a key element in the modern detective story. Without deduction, there can be little true detection, only accidental revelation. Deduction involves the discovery of the true character of an unseen or unknown condition by the process of reasoning from objective evidence.

Readers of detective novels know that in fiction as well as in fact, detection and deduction are two separate but inextricably linked processes. Detection is the long trail of discoveries and deductions that finally results in the act of exposure, or "detection," of the person responsible for the crime. Deduction is a *part* of the process of detection, usually the determination of an elusive or unknown fact that becomes a link in the chain leading to detection.

Evidence, an important element of the deductive process, consists of data by which the investigator, or detective, bridges unknowns and surmises the hidden truth. Such evidence can be information in the form of oral communication, written material, or physical objects (like footprints, a smoking gun, or Watson's tan).

Integral to the process of deduction is the crucial observable sign, or evidence, that becomes a "clue." The word comes from Middle English, *clewe*, meaning a ball of thread, yarn, or cord. The etymology of the word recalls the story of Theseus, who escaped the Labyrinth after slaying the minotaur by following his lover Ariadne's thread, which he had unwound on his way in.

Thus the clue is a key piece of evidence that leads the investigator through intricate obstacles toward the solution of a problem. Watson's tan and his injury form clues for Holmes's deduction, which actually is based on his knowledge of current events.

Not all deductions are necessarily correct ones. The accurate deduction is the linking of irrefutable facts with solid logic. Quite possibly Watson could have responded to Holmes:

"I have never been in Afghanistan. I served in the military, was invalided out, and took a post as a ship's doctor. We were marooned in the South Seas, where I was injured and became seriously ill. I was rescued only a month ago."

In fact, incorrect deduction, or false syllogism, is as important to the detective story as correct deduction. The reasoning may not be flawed so much as the evidence artfully tampered with to mislead the investigator. Such misleading clues may be deliberately planted by the criminal, or may be planted by the author to throw off the reader. In either case, the flawed deduction becomes a "red herring," the drawing of smoked fish across a scent to lead the hounds astray. There is yet another alternative: the flawed reasoning may be the result of the investigator's erroneous assumption. All are legitimate elements of the mystery genre.

It is in the second, or minor, premise of the syllogism that true deductive genius excels. Holmes knows the British have been fighting in Afghanistan; this leads him to elucidate his conclusion, deduced from his evidential observations *and* his knowledge. Had Holmes read in the newspaper a story about the rescue of a ship's crew in the South Seas, he might have come up with another deduction that would have fit an alternate set of facts about Watson.

Not only a wide knowledge of current events, or even an extensive store of esoterica makes the true deductive genius function effectively. He must have a limitless knowledge of human nature as well, plus a knowledge of scientific principles of inanimate objects as well as animate objects. In early classic literature, individuals who live by their wits—"sharpers" in the cant of the time—continually confound their contemporaries with knowledge of situations beyond their immediate observation. Again, it is their ability to utilize that crucial *second* premise as a bridge to the "astounding" deduction that makes them memorable.

The application of deductive logic to a problem fascinates the observer because the second step in the chain is never visible to the eye of the beholder. Holmes's reasoning is more exciting left in abeyance for the time being—*and brought forward later.* The brilliant leap over that second step in logic is the element that eternally fascinates the reader.

In assembling this collection of works containing deductive elements, chronological order has been observed to give the reader a feeling of the gradual appreciation for deduction in detection perceived by writers through centuries of literary development.

For example, the first stories, from Herodotus's history and the book of Daniel in the *Apocrypha,* deal with deductions made from simple observation of evidence—inferences that solved, or tried to solve, criminal acts. In the material from the *Arabian Nights*—two thousand years later—deductive talents in the characters are used in a more subtle manner, with interesting results.

By the time Voltaire's *Zadig* appeared, deduction was being used for an entirely different effect; the focus of the literary world had shifted from the Near East to France, where deduction, reason, and intellectualism were increasing rapidly in the Age of Enlightenment.

The middle selections, embracing the first half of the nineteenth century, deal with literary applications of deduction, some inspired by cases from real life. In the skilled literary hands of E.T.A. Hoffmann, the German storyteller, Edward Bulwer-Lytton, the English author-politician, and Alexandre Dumas, the French master of the swashbuckler, story materials dealing with deduction have become more subtle and imaginative. While actual scenes of deduction appear, they occur only as specific incidents rather than as the central core of the story line. Nevertheless, these examples foreshadow the modern detective genre.

It was left to two individuals to make the breakthrough to the detective story per se.

One was Edgar Allan Poe, the American poet who was forced to turn to editing and writing prose to make a living, and Eugène François Vidocq, a professional thief who became a law enforcer in his maturity and established the most famous police force on the Continent, the Paris Sûreté. Poe invented the detective short story, which has remained virtually unchanged to this day; Vidocq produced a book-length study of crime in his *Mémoires*, which deals realistically with deduction in the fight for law and order.

In Poe's formula what Sherlock Holmes later called "deduction" was called "ratiocination," the Latin word for "act of reasoning." But Poe's formula contains the essential ingredient without which there could be no Golden Age of Detective Fiction—the amateur sleuth. That was his own particularized addition to the evolving composite.

In the final selections, comprising excerpts of novels and stories from 1850 to 1887, writers begin to see the possibilities in characterizing the hardworking detective on the force and in making more imaginative use of the art of deduction in moving forward their story lines.

By now the London police had emulated Paris's Sûreté by creating a detective division, inspiring Charles Dickens to create

"Inspector Bucket of the Detective" in *Bleak House*, Wilkie Collins to create Sergeant Cuff in *The Moonstone*, and Mrs. Henry Wood to invent subplots to hold her "sensational" novels together.

Even lesser writers, like the pseudonymous author of *The Notting Hill Mystery*, were attracted to the new vogue and provided excellent scenes of deduction in novels that were not totally involved in crime. In France, Emile Gaboriau, with his Lecoq and M. Absinthe, anticipated the detective genre by creating the *roman policier*, or police novel.

And so, by 1887, the stage was set for A. Conan Doyle and his detective creation, Sherlock Holmes, to bring the detective novel and detective story to full fruition.

If the roots of detection were always there throughout the many centuries of literary endeavor, it still required two men of genius— Poe and Doyle—to nurture the plant and bring it fully to life to flourish in the twentieth century as the genre we know as the detective story.

These are the roots that Doyle and Poe watered, fed, and cared for, and without which there would be no such modern literary genre at all.

BRUCE CASSIDAY

The Clue of the Headless Corpse

From *The Histories*

HERODOTUS

Translated by George Rawlinson

Called the "father of history," Herodotus (fifth century B.C.) wrote a vast and ambitious history of the ancient world after traveling extensively throughout the eastern Mediterranean area. The history contains legends, myths, and stories, in addition to facts about the Persian Wars, the Greeks, the Egyptians, and the Turks. The style of writing may seem strange to the modern reader, resembling a resumé of action rather than the full-bodied narration fleshed out with dialogue and atmosphere so familiar today. However, the bare-bones action evokes surprisingly modern characters, relationships, and intrigues.

The excerpt comes from Book II, in which Egyptian history predominates. Deduction plays an important part in this "caper"-type story of a thief whose main concern is to prevent his ultimate detection and an Egyptian king whose intent is to plug up the leak in the royal treasury. The story contains modern elements found in contemporary mysteries: the king's ruse of using his daughter as bait to catch the thief, the thief's device of getting the guards tipsy to allow him to outwit them; and even the surprise ending in which craft

7

triumphs over virtue. With the Herodotus scenario, the imaginative reader can cast James Mason (the king), Sally Field (the princess), and Burt Reynolds (the thief), and write an original modern cinema comedy of manners.

King Rhampsinitus was possessed, they said, of great riches in silver—indeed to such an amount that none of the princes, his successors, surpassed or even equaled his wealth.

For the better custody of his money, he proposed to build a vast chamber of hewn stone, one side of which was to form a part of the outer wall of his palace. The builder, therefore, having designs upon the treasures, contrived, as he was making the building, to insert in this wall a stone, which could easily be removed from its place by two men, or even by one.

So the chamber was finished, and the king's money stored away in it. Time passed, and the builder fell sick. When finding his end approaching, he called for his two sons, and related to them the contrivance he had made in the king's treasure-chamber, telling them it was for their sakes he had done it, so that they might always live in affluence.

Then he gave them clear directions concerning the mode of removing the stone, and communicated the measurements, bidding them carefully keep the secret, whereby they would be Comptrollers of the Royal Exchequer so long as they lived. Then the father died, and the sons were not slow in setting to work. They went by night to the palace, found the stone in the wall of the building, and having removed it with ease, plundered the treasury of a round sum.

When the king next paid a visit to the apartment, he was astonished to see that the money was sunk in some of the vessels wherein it was stored away. Whom to accuse, however, he knew not, as the seals were all perfect, and the fastenings of the room secure. Still each time that he repeated his visits, he found that more money was gone. The thieves in truth never stopped, but plundered the treasury ever more and more.

At last the king determined to have some traps made, and set near the vessels which contained his wealth. This was done, and when the thieves came, as usual, to the treasure-chamber, and one of them entering through the aperture, made straight for the jars, suddenly he found himself caught in one of the traps.

Perceiving that he was lost, he instantly called his brother, and telling him what had happened, entreated him to enter as quickly as possible and cut off his head, that when his body should be discovered it might not be recognized, which would have the effect of bringing ruin upon both. The other thief thought the advice good, and was persuaded to follow it. Then, fitting the stone into its place, he went home, taking with him his brother's head.

When day dawned, the king came into the room, and marvelled greatly to see the body of the thief in the trap without a head, while the building was still whole, and neither entrance nor exit was to be seen anywhere. In his perplexity he commanded the body of the dead man to be hung up outside the palace wall, and set a guard to watch it, with orders that if any persons were seen weeping or lamenting near the place, they should be seized and brought before him.

When his mother heard of this exposure of the corpse of her son, she took it sorely to heart, and spoke to her surviving child, bidding him devise some plan or other to get back the body, and threatening, that if he did not exert himself, she would go herself to the king, and denounce him as the robber.

The son said all he could to persuade her to let the matter rest, but in vain. She still continued to trouble him, until at last he yielded to her importunity, and contrived as follows:

Filling some skins with wine, he loaded them on donkeys, which he drove before him till he came to the place where the guards were watching the dead body. When pulling two or three of the skins toward him, he untied some of the necks which dangled by the asses' sides. The wine poured freely out, whereupon he began to beat his head, and shout with all his might, seeming not to know which of the donkeys he should turn to first.

When the guards saw the wine running, delighted to profit by the occasion, they rushed out and all into the road, each with some vessel or other, and caught the liquor as it was spilling. The driver pretended anger, and loaded them with abuse, whereupon they did their best to pacify him. At last he appeared to soften and recover his good humor, drove his asses aside out of the road, and set to work to rearrange their burdens.

Meanwhile, as he talked and chatted with the guards, one of them began to rally him, and make him laugh, whereupon he gave them one of the skins as a gift. They now made up their minds to sit down and have a drinking bout where they were, so they begged him to remain and drink with them. Then the man let himself be persuaded, and stayed.

As the drinking went on, they grew very friendly together, so presently he gave them another skin, upon which they drank so copiously that they were all overcome with the liquor, and growing drowsy lay down and fell asleep on the spot.

The thief waited till it was the dead of the night, and then took down the body of his brother. After that, in mockery, he shaved off the right side of all the soldiers' beards, and so left them. Laying his brother's body upon the asses, he carried it home to his mother, having thus accomplished the thing that she had required of him.

When it came to the king's ears that the thief's body was stolen away, he was sorely vexed. Wishing, therefore, whatever it might cost, to catch the man who had contrived the trick, he had recourse, the priests said, to an expedient, which I can scarcely credit. He sent his own daughter to the common stews, with orders to admit all comers, but to require every man to tell her what was the cleverest and wickedest thing he had done in the whole course of his life. If any one in reply told her the story of the thief, she was to lay hold of him and not allow him to get away.

The daughter did as her father willed, whereon the thief, who was well aware of the king's motive, felt a desire to outdo him in craft and cunning. Accordingly he contrived the following plan:

He procured the corpse of a man lately dead, and cutting off one of the arms at the shoulder, put it under his dress, and so went to the king's daughter. When she put the question to him as she had done to all the rest, he replied that the wickedest thing he had ever done was cutting off the head of his brother when he was caught in a trap in the king's treasury, and the cleverest was making the guards drunk and carrying off the body.

As he spoke, the princess caught at him, but the thief took advantage of the darkness to hold out to her the hand of the corpse. Imagining it to be his own hand, she seized and held it fast, while the thief, leaving it in her grasp, made his escape by the door.

The king, when word was brought him of this fresh success, amazed at the sagacity and boldness of the man, sent messengers to all the towns in his dominions to proclaim a free pardon for the thief, and to promise him a rich reward, if he came and made himself known.

The thief took the king at his word, and came boldly into his presence. Thereupon Rhampsinitus, greatly admiring him, and looking on him as the most knowing of men, gave him his daughter in marriage.

"The Egyptians," he said, "excelled all the rest of the world in wisdom, and this man excelled all other Egyptians."

The Priests of Bel

From the *Book of Daniel*

FOUND IN THE *APOCRYPHA*

The biblical prophet Daniel (sixth century B.C.) lived in Mesopotamia, where in court circles he was known by the name of "Belteshazzar." A shrewd observer of people and politics, he made his name in wily interpretations of "signs"—particularly the dreams of Nebuchadnezzar, even correctly predicting the king's imminent madness. Using deductive methods of his own, he "decoded" the mysterious writing on the wall at Belshazzar's feast, and even warned of the coming apocalypse in four separate "visions." Daniel's prognostications were actually carefully worded extrapolations of events and people—his own "deductions" about the way things would work out in the future, given the present facts.

In the selection here from the Greek version of the Bible (first century B.C.), dropped from the King James version as part of the *Apocrypha* (literally, "hidden away" because of dubious authenticity), Daniel acts more in the manner of a detective than a popular pollster. He deduces that Bel, worshipped by the Persians, is not a true god, but simply an idol set up by human agency. The way he proves it to the king and trips up the false priests is an early example of a very modern detective story.

...3 Now the Babylonians had an idol, called Bel, and there were spent upon him every day twelve measures of fine flour, and forty sheep, and six vessels of wine.

4   And the king worshipped it, and went daily to adore it: but Daniel worshipped his own God. And the king said unto him, Why dost not thou worship Bel?

5   Who answered and said, Because I may not worship idols made with hands, but the living God, who hath created the heaven and the earth, and hath sovereignty over all flesh.

6   Then said the king unto him, Thinkest thou not that Bel is a living god? seest thou not how much he eateth and drinketh every day?

7   Then Daniel smiled, and said, O king, be not deceived: for this is but clay within and brass without, and did never eat or drink any thing.

8   So the king was wroth, and called for his priests, and said unto them, If ye tell me not who this is that devoureth these expenses ye shall die.

9   But if ye can certify me that Bel devoureth them, then Daniel shall die: for he hath spoken blasphemy against Bel. And Daniel said unto the king, Let it be according to thy word.

10   Now the priests of Bel were threescore and ten, besides their wives and children. And the king went with Daniel into the temple of Bel.

11   So Bel's priests said, Lo, we go out: but thou, O king, set on the meat, and make ready the wine, and shut the door fast, and seal it with thine own signet;

12   And to-morrow when thou comest in, if thou findest not that Bel hath eaten up all, we will suffer death; or else Daniel, that speaketh falsely against us.

13   And they little regarded it: for under the table they had made privy entrance, whereby they entered in continually, and consumed those things.

14   So when they were gone forth, the king set meats before Bel. Now Daniel had commanded his servants to bring ashes, and those they strewed throughout all the temple in the presence of the king alone: then went they out and shut the door, and sealed it with the king's signet, and so departed.

15   Now in the night came the priests with their wives and children, as they were wont to do, and did eat and drink up all.

16   In the morning betimes the king arose, and Daniel with him.

17   And the king said, Daniel, are the seals whole? And he said, Yea, O king, they be whole.

18   And as soon as he had opened the door, the king looked upon the table, and cried with a loud voice, Great art thou, O Bel, and with thee is no deceit at all.

19   Then laughed Daniel, and held the king that he should not go in, and said, Behold now the pavement, and mark well whose footsteps are these.

20   And the king said, I see the footsteps of men, women, and children. And then the king was angry,

21   And took the priests with their wives and children, who showed him the privy doors, where they came in, and consumed such things as were upon the table.

22   Therefore the king slew them, and delivered Bel into Daniel's power, who destroyed him and his temple.

The Three Sharpers

From *The Arabian Nights*

Translated by Sir Richard Burton

The Arabian Nights, or *The Thousand and One Nights,* as the
collection became popularly known, appeared in various
translations and treatments, most of them in Europe during
the late seventeenth century. The tales included adventure
stories, romances, popular myths, anecdotes, and all manner
of fictional representations. "Ali Baba and the Forty
Thieves," "The Travels of Sinbad the Sailor," and dozens
of other stories became a part of man's continuing culture.
By the nineteenth century most of the stories had been
borrowed and altered in different ways. Scholars began
returning to the original material for more accurate translations. Sir Richard F. Burton (1821–1890) supplied one of
the most literate and entertaining versions of the collection
in the late nineteenth century. Throwing aside bowdlerized
earlier versions, Burton went to the heart of the material,
leaving out nothing, and writing in an imitation of Middle
English prose for flavor.

In the excerpt here, which appears in Burton's *Sup-
plement* (1888), the hero is the man who lives by his wits,
called the "sharper" in the jargon of the time. Always a
popular folk hero, the sharper rises by his innate cunning. In
"The Three Sharpers" a trio of slickers try to outdo one
another in solving problems assigned them by the king/
sultan who has the power of life and death over them. The
cleverest at deduction and accurate penetration of the truth
wins out in the end.

There were in time of yore three sharpers who were wont every day in early morning to prowl forth and to prey, rummaging among the mounds which outlay the city.

Therein each would find a silver bit of five parahs or its equivalent, after which the trio would foregather and buy whatso sufficed them for supper. They would also expend two half-dirhams upon bast, which is bhang [hashish], and purchase a waxen taper with the other silver bit.

They had hired a cell in the flank of a wakalah, a caravansary without the walls, where they could sit at ease to solace themselves and eat their hashish after lighting the candle, and enjoy their intoxication and consequent merriment till the noon o' night.

Then they would sleep, again awaking at day-dawn when they would arise and seek for spoil, according to their custom, and ransack the heaps where at times they would hit upon a silvering of five dirhams and at other times a piece of four. And at eventide they would meet to spend together the dark hours, and they would expend everything they came by every day.

For a length of time they pursued this path until, one day of the days, they made for the mounds as was their wont and went round searching the heaps from morning to evening without finding even a half-parah. Wherefore they were troubled and they went away and nighted in their cell without meat or drink.

When the next day broke they arose and repaired for booty, changing the places wherein they were wont to forage. But none of them found aught, and their breasts were straitened for lack of a find of dirhams wherewith to buy them supper.

This lasted for three full-told and following days until hunger waxed hard upon them and vexation. So they said one to other, "Go we to the sultan and let us serve him with a sleight, and each of us three shall claim to be a past master of some craft. Haply Allah Almighty may incline his heart uswards and he may largesse us with something to expend upon our necessities."

Accordingly all three agreed to do on this wise and they sought the sultan whom they found in the palace-garden. They asked leave to go in to him, but the chamberlains refused admission. So they stood afar off unable to approach the presence.

Then quoth they one to other, "'Twere better we fall to and

each smite his comrade and cry aloud and make a clamor, and as soon as he shall hear us he will send to summon us."

Accordingly they jostled one another and each took to frapping his fellow, making the while loud outcries.

The sultan, hearing this turmoil, said, "Bring me yonder wights."

And the chamberlains and eunuchs ran out to them and seized them and set them between the hands of the sovereign.

As soon as they stood in the presence, he asked them, "What be the cause of your wrath one against other?"

They answered, "O King of the Age, we are past masters of crafts, each of us weeting an especial art."

Quoth the sultan, "What be your crafts?"

Quoth one of the trio, "O our Lord, as for my art I am a jeweler by trade."

The king exclaimed, "Passing strange! A sharper and a jeweler. This is a wondrous matter." And he questioned the second sharper, saying, "And thou, the other, what may be thy craft?"

He answered, "I am a genealogist of the horse-kind."

So the king glanced at him in surprise and said to himself, "A sharper, yet he claimeth an astounding knowledge!" Then he left him and put the same question to the third, who said to him, "O King of the Age, verily my art is more wondrous and marvelous than aught thou hast heard from these twain. Their craft is easy, but mine is such that none save I can discover the right direction thereto or know the first of it from the last of it."

The sultan inquired of him, "And what be thy craft?"

Whereto he replied, "My craft is the genealogy of the sons of Adam."

Hearing these words the sovereign wondered with extreme wonderment and said in himself, "Verily He informeth with His secrets the humblest of His creatures! Assuredly these men, an they speak truth in all they say and it prove soothfast, are fit for naught except kingship. But I will keep them by me until the occurrence of some nice contingency wherein I may test them. Then, if they approve themselves good men and trustworthy of word, I will leave them on life. But if their speech be lying I will do them die."

Upon this he set apart for them apartments and rationed them with three cakes of bread and a dish of roast meat and set over them his sentinels dreading lest they fly. This case continued for a while till behold, there came to the sultan from the land of 'Ajam a present of rarities, among which were two gems whereof one was clear of water and the other was clouded of color.

The sultan hent them in hand for a time and fell to considering them straitly for the space of an hour. After that he called to mind the first of the three sharpers, the self-styled jeweler, and cried, "Bring me the jeweler-man."

Accordingly they went and brought him and set him before the sovereign who asked him, "O man, art thou a lapidary?"

And when the sharper answered, "Yes," he gave him the clear-watered stone, saying, "What may be the price of this gem?"

Then the sharper took the jewel in hand and turned it rightward and leftward and considered the outside and pried into the inside, after which he said to the sultan, "O my lord, verily this gem containeth a worm bred within the heart thereof."

Now when the king heard these words he waxed wroth with exceeding wrath and commanded the man's head to be stricken off, saying, "This jewel is clear of color and free of flaw or other default. Yet thou chargest it falsely with containing a worm!"

Then he summoned the linkman who laid hands on the sharper and pinioned his elbows and trussed up his legs like a camel's and was about to smite his neck when behold, the wazir entered the presence and, seeing the sovereign in high dudgeon and the sharper under the scimiter, asked what was to do.

The sultan related to him what had happened, when he drew near to him and said, "O my lord, act not after this fashion! An thou determine upon the killing of yonder man, first break the gem and, if thou find therein a worm, thou wilt know the wight's word to have been veridical. But an thou find it sound then strike off his head."

"Right is thy rede," quoth the king. Then he took in hand the gem and smote it with his mace and when it brake behold, he found therein the worm amiddlemost thereof.

So he marveled at the sight and asked the man, "What proved to thee that it harbored a worm?"

"The sharpness of my sight," answered the sharper.

Then the sultan pardoned him, and, admiring his power of vision, addressed his attendants, saying, "Bear him back to his comrades and ration him with a dish of roast meat and two cakes of bread."

And they did as he bade them.

After some time, on a day of the days, there came to the king the tribute of 'Ajam-land accompanied with presents, amongst which was a colt whose robe black as night showed one shade in the sun and another in the shadow. When the animal was displayed to the sultan he fell in love with it and set apart for it a stall and solaced himself at all times by gazing at it, and was wholly occupied with it and sang its praises till they filled the whole countryside.

Presently he remembered the sharper who claimed to be a genealogist of the horse-kind and bade him be summoned. So they fared forth and brought him and set him between the hands of the sovereign who said to him, "Art thou he who knoweth the breed and descent of horses?"

"Yea verily," said the man.

Then cried the king, "By the truth of Him who set me upon the necks of His servants and who sayeth to a thing 'Be' and it becometh, an I find aught of error or confusion in thy words, I will strike off thy head."

"Harkening and obedience," quoth the sharper.

Then they led him to the colt that he might consider its genealogy. They called aloud to the groom, and when they brought him he bade the stirrup-holder back the colt for his inspection. So he mounted the animal and made it pace to the right and to the left, causing it now to prance and curvet and then to step leisurely, while the connoisseur looked on and after a time quoth he to the groom, "'Tis enough!"

Then he went in to the presence and stood between the hands of the king who inquired, "What has thou seen in the colt, O Kashmar?"

Replied the sharper, "By Allah, O King of the Age, this colt is of pure and noble blood on the side of the sire. Its action is excellent and all its qualities are praiseworthy save one. And but for this one it had been perfect in blood and breed nor had there been on earth's face its fellow in horseflesh. But its blemish remaineth a secret."

The sultan asked, "And what is the quality which thou blamest?" and the sharper answered:

"Its sire was noble, but its dam was of other strain. She it was that brought the blemish and if thou, O my lord, allow me I will notify it to thee."

"'Tis well, and needs must thou declare it," quoth the sultan. Then said the sharper, "Its dam is a buffalo-cow [mule]."

When the king heard these words he was wroth with wrath exceeding and he bade the linkman take the sharper and behead him, crying, "O dog! O accursed! How can a buffalo-cow bear a horse?"

The sharper replied, "O my lord, the linkman is in the presence. But send and fetch him who brought thee the colt and of him make inquiry. If my words prove true and rightly placed, my skill shall be stablished. But an they be lies, let my head pay forfeit for my tongue. Here standeth the linkman and I am between thy hands. Thou hast but to bid him strike off my head!"

Thereupon the king sent for the owner and breeder of the colt and they brought him to the presence. And the sultan asked him, saying, "Tell me the truth anent the blood of this colt. Didst thou buy it or breed it so that it was a rearling of thy homestead?"

Said he, "By Allah, O King of the Age, I will speak naught which is not sooth, for indeed there hangeth by this colt the strangest story. Were it graven with graver-needles upon the eye-corners it had been a warning to whoso would be warned. And this it is. I had a stallion of purest strain whose sire was of the steeds of the sea. And he was stabled in a stall apart for fear of the evil eye, his service being entrusted to trusty servants. But one day in springtide the syce [groom] took the horse into the open and there picketed him when behold, a buffalo-cow walked into the enclosed pasture where the stallion was tethered, and seeing her he brake his heel-ropes and rushed at her and covered her.

"She conceived by him and when her days were completed and her throwing-time came, she suffered sore pains and bare yonder colt. And all who have seen it or have heard of it were astounded," said he, presently adding, "By Allah, O King of the Age, had its dam been the mare-kind, the colt would have had no equal on earth's surface or aught approaching it."

Hereat the sultan took thought and marveled. Then, summoning the sharper he said to him when present, "O man, thy speech is true and thou art indeed a genealogist in horseflesh and thou wottest it well. But I would know what proved to thee that the dam of this colt was a buffalo-cow?"

Said he, "O King, my proof thereof was palpable, nor can it be concealed from any wight of right wits and intelligence and special knowledge. For the horse's hoof is round while the hooves of buffaloes are elongated and duck-shaped, and hereby I kenned that this colt was a jumart, the issue of a cow-buffalo."

The sultan was pleased with his words and said, "Ration him with a plate of roast meat and two cakes of bread." And they did as they were bidden.

Now for a length of time the third sharper was forgotten till one day the sultan bethought him of the man who could explain the genealogy of Adam's sons. So he bade fetch him and when they brought him into the presence he said, "Thou art he that knowest the caste and descent of men and women?"

And the other said, "Yes."

Then he commanded the eunuchs take him to his wife and place him before her and cause him declare her genealogy. So they led him in and set him standing in her presence, and the sharper considered her for awhile, looking from right to left. Then he fared forth to the sultan who asked him, "What has thou seen in the Queen?"

Answered he, "O my lord, I saw a somewhat adorned with loveliness and beauty and perfect grace, with fair stature of symmetrical trace and with modesty and fine manners and skilful case. And she is one in whom all good qualities appear on every side, nor is aught of accomplishments or knowledge concealed from her, and haply in her center all desirable attributes. Natheless, O King of the Age, there is a curious point that dishonoreth her, from the which were she free none would outshine her of all the women of her generation."

Now when the sultan heard the words of the sharper, he sprang hastily to his feet and clapping hand upon hilt bared his brand [sword] and fell upon the man, purposing to slay him. But the chamberlains and the eunuchs prevented him, saying, "O our lord, kill him not until his falsehood or his fact shall have been made manifest to thee."

The sultan said to him, "What then appeared to thee in my queen?"

"She is ferly fair," said the man, "but her mother is a dancing-girl, a gypsy."

The fury of the king increased hereat and he sent to summon the inmates of his harem and cried to his father-in-law, "Unless thou speak me sooth concerning thy daughter and her descent and her mother, I—"

He replied, "By Allah, O King of the Age, naught saveth a man save soothfastness! Her mother indeed was a ghaziyah [gypsy]. In past time a part of the tribe was passing by my abode when a young maid strayed from her fellows and was lost. They asked no questions concerning her, so I lodged her and bred her in my homestead till she grew up to be a great girl and the fairest of her time. My heart would not brook her wiving with any other, so I wedded her and she bare me this daughter whom thou, O King, has espoused."

When the sultan heard these words the flame in his heart was quenched [because the gypsy had not been a "dancing-girl," euphemism for public prostitute] and he wondered at the subtlety of the sharper man. So he summoned him and asked him, saying, "O wily one, tell me what certified to thee that my Queen had a dancing-girl, a gypsy, to mother?"

He answered, "O King of the Age, verily the Ghaziyah race hath eye-balls intensely black and bushy brows, whereas other women than the Ghaziyah have the reverse of this."

On such wise the king was convinced of the man's skill and he cried, "Ration him with a dish of roast meat and two scones."

They did as he bade and the three sharpers tarried with the sultan a long time till one day when the king said to himself, "Verily these three men have by their skill solved every question of genealogy which I proposed to them. First the jeweler proved his perfect knowledge of gems. Secondly the genealogist of the horse-kind showed himself as skilful. And the same was the case with the genealogist of mankind, for he discovered the origin of my queen and the truth of his words appeared from all quarters. Now 'tis my desire that he do the same with me that I also may know my provenance."

Accordingly they set the man between his hands and he said to him, "O fellow, hast thou the power to tell me mine origin?"

Said the sharper, "Yes, O my lord, I can trace thy descent, but I will so do only upon a condition—to wit, that thou promise me safety after what I shall have told them. For the saw saith, 'Whilst sultan sitteth on throne 'ware his despite, inasmuch as none may be contumacious when he saith 'Smite.'"

Thereupon the sultan told him, "Thou hast a promise of immunity, a promise which shall never be falsed."

And the man said, "O King of the Age, whenas I acquaint thee
with thy root and branch, let it be between us twain lest these present
hear us."

"Wherefore O man?" asked the sultan, and the sharper answered:

"O my lord, Allah of Allmight hath among His names 'The
Veiler.'"

Wherefore the king bade his chamberlains and eunuchs retire so
that none remained in the place save those two.

Then the sharper came forward and said, "O my lord, thou art a
son of shame and an issue of adultery."

As soon as the king heard these words, his case changed and his
color waxed wan and his limbs fell loose. He foamed at the mouth.
He lost hearing and sight. He became as one drunken without wine,
and he fell fainting to the ground.

After awhile he recovered and said to the sharper, "Now by the
truth of Him who hath set me upon the necks of His servants, an thy
words be veridical and I ascertain their sooth by proof positive, I will
assuredly abdicate my kingdom and resign my realm to thee, because
none deserveth it save thou and it becometh us least of all and every.
But an I find thy speech lying, I will slay thee."

He replied, "Hearing and obeying."

And the sovereign, rising up without stay or delay, went inside
to his mother with grip on glaive [sword], and said to her, "By the
truth of Him who uplifted the life above the earth, an thou answer me
not with the whole truth in whatso I ask thee, I will cut thee to little
bits with this blade."

She inquired, "What dost thou want with me?"

And he replied, "Whose son am I, and what may be my
descent?"

She rejoined, "Although falsehood be an excuse, fact and truth
are superior and more saving. Thou art indeed the very son of a cook.
The sultan that was before thee took me to wife and I cohabited with
him awhile of time without my becoming pregnant by him or having
issue. And he would mourn and groan from the core of his heart for
that he had no seed, nor girl nor boy. Neither could he enjoy aught of
sweet food or sleep.

"Now we had about the palace many caged birds. And at last,
one day of the days, the king longed to eat somewhat of poultry, so
he went into the court and sent for the kitchener to slaughter one of

the fowls. And the man applied himself to catching it. At that time I had taken my first bath after the monthly ailment and quoth I to myself, 'If this case continue with the king, he will perish and the kingdom pass from us.' And the Shaytan [Satan] tempted me to that which displeased Allah, making the sin fair in my sight.

"So I went up to the kitchener, attired and adorned as I was in my finest apparel, and I fell a-jesting with him, and provoking him, and disporting with him till his passions were excited by me. So he tumbled me at that very hour, after which he arose and slaughtered one of the birds and went his ways.

"Then I bade the handmaids sprinkle water on the fowl and clean it and cook it, and they did my bidding. After awhile symptoms of pregnancy declared themselves in me and became evident. And when the king heard that his queen was with child, he waxed gladsome and joyful and gave alms and scattered gifts and bestowed robes upon his officers of estate and others, till the day of my delivery. And I bore a babe—which is thyself.

"Now at that time the sultan was hunting and birding and enjoying himself about the gardens, all of his pleasure at the prospect of becoming a father, and when the bearer of good news went to him and announced the birth of a man-child, he hurried back to me and forthright bade them decorate the capital and he found the report true. So the city adorned itself for forty days in honor of its king. Such is my case and my tale."

Thereupon the king went forth from her to the sharper and bade him doff his dress, and when this had been done, he doffed his own raiment and habited the man in royal gear and hooded him with the taylasan hood, and asked him, saying, "What proof hast thou of my being a son of adultery?"

The sharper answered, "O my lord, my proof was thy bidding our being rationed, after showing the perfection of our skill, with a dish of roast meat and two scones of bread. Whereby I knew thee to be of cook's breed, for the kings be wont in such case to make presents of money and valuables, not of meat and bread as thou didst, and this evidenced thee to be a bastard king."

He replied, "Sooth thou sayest," and then robed him with the rest of his robes including the kalansuwah, or royal head-dress, under the hood, and seating him upon the throne of his estate, went forth from him after abandoning all his women to him and assumed the garb of a darwaysh [dervish] who wandereth about the world, and formally abdicated his dominion to his successor.

But when the sharper-king saw himself in this condition, he reflected and said to himself, "Summon thy whilome comrades and see whether they recognize thee or not."

So he caused them be set before him and conversed with them. Then, perceiving that none knew him, he gifted them and sent them to gang their gait.

And he ruled his realm and bade and forbade and gave and took away and was gracious and generous to each and every of his lieges, so that the people of that region who were his subjects blessed him and prayed for him.

The Dog and the Horse

From *Zadig*

VOLTAIRE

Translated by Tobias Smollett

François Marie Arouet, otherwise known as Voltaire (1694–1778), began his literary career writing tragedies and epics while serving in the Bastille for intellectual offenses against Philippe II d'Orleans, regent of France. Freed again, he won an enormous amount of money in a public lottery and acquired a handsome fortune after successfully speculating with his winnings; he died a millionaire. His masterpiece was most assuredly *Candide* (1759), in which he satirized the complicated philosophical studies of the time, and proposed a substitute of common sense and down-to-earth realism in place of the blind optimism of popular thinkers like Gottfried von Leibniz (1646–1716).

Among Voltaire's best-known philosophical romances is *Zadig* (1747), a brilliant spoof on the popularity of the *Arabian Nights*. His aim in *Zadig* is not to tell a tale to parallel the oriental romances of the time, but to satirize the inconvenience of reason in what he saw to be an essentially unreasoning age. Zadig's genius at deduction, in Voltaire's view, is a definite handicap. Although his tongue is well embedded in his cheek in the chapter taken from the book, this tale of wit and wisdom has a grace and a bounce that is typical of Voltaire's truly imaginative literary genius.

Zadig found by experience that the first month of marriage, as it is written in the book of Zend, is the moon of honey, and that the second is the moon of wormwood. He was some times after obliged to repudiate Azora, who became too difficult to be pleased; and he then sought for happiness in the study of nature.

"No man," said he, "can be happier than a philosopher who reads in this great book which God hath placed before our eyes. The truths he discovers are his own, he nourishes and exalts his soul; he lives in peace; he fears nothing from men; and his tender spouse will not come to cut off his nose."

Possessed of these ideas he retired to a country house on the banks of the Euphrates. There he did not employ himself in calculating how many inches of water flow in a second of time under the arches of a bridge, or whether there fell a cubelin of rain in the month of the Mouse more than in the month of the Sheep. He never dreamed of making silk of cobwebs, or porcelain of broken bottles; but he chiefly studied the properties of plants and animals; and soon acquired a sagacity that made him discover a thousand differences where other men see nothing but uniformity.

One day, as he was walking near a little wood, he saw one of the queen's eunuchs running toward him, followed by several officers, who appeared to be in great perplexity, and who ran to and fro like men distracted, eagerly searching for something they had lost of great value.

"Young man," said the first eunuch, "hast thou seen the queen's dog?"

"It is a female," replied Zadig.

"Thou are in the right," returned the first eunuch.

"It is a very small she spaniel," added Zadig; "she has lately whelped; she limps on the left forefoot, and has very long ears."

"Thou has seen her," said the first eunuch, quite out of breath.

"No," replied Zadig, "I have not seen her, nor did I so much as know that the queen had a dog."

Exactly at the same time, by one of the common freaks of fortune, the first horse in the king's stable had escaped from the jockey in the plains of Babylon. The principal huntsman and all the other officers ran after him with as much eagerness and anxiety as the first eunuch had done after the spaniel.

The principal huntsman addressed himself to Zadig, and asked him if he had not seen the king's horse passing by.

"He is the fleetest horse in the king's stable," replied Zadig; "he is five feet high, with very small hoofs, and a tail three feet and a half in length; the studs on his bit are gold of twenty-three carats, and his shoes are silver of eleven pennyweights."

"What way did he take? where is he?" demanded the chief huntsman.

"I have not seen him," replied Zadig, "and never heard talk of him before."

The principal huntsman and the first eunuch never doubted but that Zadig had stolen the king's horse and the queen's spaniel. They therefore had him conducted before the assembly of the grand desterham, who condemned him to the knout, and to spend the rest of his days in Siberia.

Hardly was the sentence passed when the horse and the spaniel were both found. The judges were reduced to the disagreeable necessity of reversing their sentence; but they condemned Zadig to pay four hundred ounces of gold for having said that he had not seen what he had seen. This fine he was obliged to pay; after which he was permitted to plead his cause before the counsel of the grand desterham, when he spoke to the following effect:

"Ye stars of justice, abyss of sciences, mirrors of truth, who have the weight of lead, the hardness of iron, the splendor of the diamond, and many properties of gold: Since I am permitted to speak before this august assembly, I swear to you by Oramades that I have never seen the queen's respectable spaniel, nor the sacred horse of the king of kings. The truth of the matter was as follows: I was walking toward the little wood, where I afterwards met the venerable eunuch, and the most illustrious chief huntsman.

"I observed on the sand the traces of an animal, and could easily perceive them to be those of a little dog. The light and long furrows impressed on little eminences of sand between the marks of the paws plainly discovered that it was a female, whose dugs were hanging down, and that therefore she must have whelped a few days before. Other traces of a different kind, that always appeared to have gently brushed the surface of the sand near the marks of the forefeet, showed me that she had very long ears; and as I remarked that there was always a slighter impression made on the sand by one foot than the other three, I found that the spaniel of our august queen was a little lame, if I may be allowed the expression.

"With regard to the horse of the king of kings, you will be pleased to know that, walking in the lanes of this wood, I observed the marks of a horse's shoes, all at equal distances. This must be a horse, said I to myself, that gallops excellently. The dust on the trees in the road that was but seven feet wide was a little brushed off, at the distance of three feet and a half from the middle of the road. This horse, said I, has a tail three feet and a half long, which being whisked to the right and left, has swept away the dust. I observed under the trees that formed an arbor five feet in height, that the leaves of the branches were newly fallen; from whence I inferred that the horse had touched them, and that he must therefore be five feet high.

"As to his bit, it must be gold of twenty-three carats, for he had rubbed its bosses against a stone which I knew to be a touchstone, and which I have tried. In a word, from the marks made by his shoes on flints of another kind, I concluded that he was shod with silver eleven deniers fine."

All the judges admired Zadig for his acute and profound discernment. The news of this speech was carried even to the king and queen. Nothing was talked of but Zadig in the antichambers, the chambers, and the cabinet; and though many of the magi were of opinion that he ought to be burned as a sorcerer, the king ordered his officers to restore him the four hundred ounces of gold which he had been obliged to pay.

The register, the attorneys, and bailiffs, went to his house with great formality, to carry him back his four hundred ounces. They only retained three hundred and ninety-eight of them to defray the expenses of justice; and their servants demanded their fees.

Zadig saw how extremely dangerous it sometimes is to appear too knowing, and therefore resolved that on the next occasion of the like nature he would not tell what he had seen.

Such an opportunity soon offered. A prisoner of state made his escape, and passed under the window of Zadig's house. Zadig was examined and made no answer. But it was proved that he had looked at the prisoner from his window. For this crime he was condemned to pay five hundred ounces of gold; and, according to the polite custom of Babylon, he thanked his judges for their indulgence.

"Great God!" said he to himself, "what a misfortune it is to walk in a wood through which the queen's spaniel or the king's horse has passed! how dangerous to look out at a window! and how difficult to be happy in this life!"

Mademoiselle de Scudéry

E.T.A. HOFFMANN

Translated by Michael Bullock

Adapted by the editor

E.T.A. Hoffmann (1776–1822) was born Ernst Theodor Wilhelm Hoffmann, but changed his third name later to Amadeus in tribute to Wolfgang Amadeus Mozart, becoming "E.T.A." to opera lovers and readers alike. In his later life he turned from the composition of music to the composition of highly original "tales"—singularly bizarre, grotesque, and memorable. Offenbach's *Tales of Hoffmann* is based on three of them, one of which contains quite probably the first appearance of today's science-fiction staple, the android.

A major figure in the Romantic movement in German literature, Hoffmann created stories that combine the supernatural with the realistic. Considered by some his masterpiece, "Mademoiselle de Scudéry" (1821), here adapted, reflects his interest in mystery, in the psychological, in crime, and in detection by means of investigation and deduction. It is one of the earliest stories posing an impossible problem—the disappearance of a man through a stone wall—and a credible explanation; one of the first to recognize the importance of modus operandi in solving a crime; and a curious example of the use of a primitive version of the "bullet-proof vest." As a bonus, it even provides a certain amount of psychological insight into twisted human motivation, preceding, by some seventy years, the writing of Sigmund Freud.

It is interesting to note that Hoffmann assigns the function of deduction and investigation to secondary characters in the story, rather than letting the title character, Mademoiselle de Scudéry, do the intuitive work that would be assigned to Miss Marple or Harriet Vane some hundred years later.

Madeleine de Scudéry, who was renowned in seventeenth-century France for her charming verses and novels, lived in a little house in the Rue Saint-Honoré, maintained for her by Louis XIV and the Marquise de Maintenon.

One midnight in the autumn of 1680 a loud knocking at the door echoed through the entrance hall. Baptiste, the cook, footman, and doorkeeper of the household, had been given permission to go to the country to attend his sister's wedding. Martinière, the chambermaid, was the only person awake in the Scudéry house.

She heard the repeated knocking and called to mind all the robberies and murders ever committed in Paris and felt sure that some pack of ruffians was furiously seeking admittance to assault her mistress. She stayed in her room, shaking with fright.

"Open the door, in the name of Christ, open the door!" called a male voice outside.

Terrified, Martinière took a lighted candlestick and hurried into the hall. "No robber would speak so," she thought. "It may be some honest fugitive seeking refuge with my mistress, who is always disposed to acts of mercy. But let us be cautious."

She opened a window and, in a voice as deep and masculine as she could make it, asked who was there. In a glimmer of moonlight she made out a tall figure wrapped in a pale-gray cloak with a broad-brimmed hat pulled down over the eyes.

"Baptiste, Claude, Pierre! Get up and see what good-for-nothing is trying to batter down our door!"

"Oh, Martinière," said a voice from below. "I know it is you, dear lady, however much you try to disguise your voice, and I know

that Baptiste has gone to the country and that you and your mistress
are alone in the house. Let me in. You have nothing to fear. I must
speak to your mistress without delay."

"What makes you think my mistress will talk to you in the
middle of the night?" Martinière demanded. "Nothing would induce
me to wake her from the first and sweetest sleep."

"I know that your mistress has just put aside the manuscript of
her novel *Clélie*, on which she has been tirelessly working, and is now
copying out some verses which she intends to lay before the
Marquise de Maintenon tomorrow. I beg you, Martinière, have
mercy and let me in. It is a question of saving an unfortunate from
perdition. My honor and freedom, indeed my very life, depend upon
my speaking to your mistress immediately."

"But why do you appeal to my lady's pity at this unusual hour?
Come early tomorrow morning."

"Does fate respect the time of day when it strikes like lightning?
Can help be delayed when only a moment is left? Open the door and
let me in!"

Martinière's heart was touched and without further reflection
she fetched the key. No sooner was the door open than the cloaked
figure burst in, strode past her, and cried wildly: "Take me to your
mistress!"

Martinière raised the candlestick. Its light fell upon the deathly
pale, fearfully contorted face of a young man. He tore open his cloak
to reveal the gleaming handle of a stiletto at his breast. "Take me to
your mistress, I tell you!"

All Martinière's love for her kindly employer blazed up in her
heart. She slammed shut the door and stood with her back to it.
"Your frenzied behavior inside does not tally with your lamentations
uttered outside. My mistress must not and will not speak to you now.
Leave the house!"

The man uttered a deep sigh, then reached for his stiletto.
Martinière stood firm.

"Let me go to your mistress," he said again.

"I will not move from this spot. Complete the evil deed you
have begun. You too will die an ignominious death in the Place de
Grève, like your villainous accomplices."

"Ha!" shouted the intruder. "I look and am armed like a
villainous robber and murderer, but my accomplices have *not* been
executed!"

"Jesus!" she screamed, awaiting the death blow. At that moment the rattle of weapons and the clatter of horses' hooves could be heard outside. "La Maréchaussée, La Maréchaussée! Help, help!" cried Martinière. La Maréchaussée was composed of Paris police who patrolled the streets at night.

"Abominable woman, you are determined to ruin me!" cried the intruder. "Take this, give it to your mistress tonight—or tomorrow, if you wish." The stranger tore the candlestick from Martinière, put out the candles, and pressed a small casket into her hands. "As you wish for salvation, give your mistress this casket!"

He raced to the door.

Martinière groped her way through the darkness back to her room, where she dropped into an armchair in a state bordering on prostration. Then she heard someone turning the key she had left in the front door. Frozen with fear, she awaited the worst. The door opened...and she recognized honest Baptiste! He looked deathly pale and greatly upset.

"In the name of all the saints," he began. "What has happened? Some terrible fear, I do not know of what, drove me away from the wedding yesterday evening. On the street just now I was met by a powerful police patrol, some on horseback and some on foot, all armed to the teeth. They stopped me and refused to let me go. But as luck would have it, Lieutenant Desgrais, a high officer in the Maréchaussée, was with them, and he knows me very well.

"'What are you doing, Baptiste, coming back in the middle of the night? You should stay at home like a good lad and look after the house. It isn't safe around here. We're expecting to make a catch tonight.'

"You can imagine, Madame Martinière, how these words pierced my heart. Then I stepped onto the threshold and a cloaked man clutching a stiletto rushed out of the house and knocked me down. The house was open, the keys in the door—tell me, what does it all mean?"

Martinière told him all that had happened. She and Baptiste then went into the hall. They found the candlestick on the floor, where the stranger had hurled it.

"There can be no doubt that our mistress was to have been robbed and probably murdered," Baptiste reasoned. "As you told me, the man knew that you were alone with Mademoiselle and even that she was still sitting up over her writing. He was undoubtedly one of those accursed rogues who break into houses, spy out the lie of the land, and note everything that may assist them in their evil designs."

After a discussion, the two servants decided to wait until next morning to tell their mistress everything and give her the mysterious casket.

Baptiste's fears were well founded. At just this period, Paris was the scene of countless dastardly atrocities. It was thought that a daring band of thieves had determined to possess all the jewels in Paris. Rich ornaments unaccountably disappeared as soon as they were bought, however carefully they were guarded. Even worse, anyone who ventured outdoors wearing jewelry in the evening was robbed, and sometimes murdered, in the open street or in the dark passages of houses. Those who escaped reported that a fist had struck them on the head and on regaining consciousness they had found themselves robbed and removed to a different place in the city. The victims of murder were to be found almost every morning lying in the street or inside houses—and all with the same fatal wound. They had been stabbed in the heart with a dagger so swiftly and surely, according to the doctors, that they must have sunk to the ground without uttering a sound.

Who, at the lascivious Court of Louis XIV, was not involved in an amorous intrigue and did not creep off to his mistress late at night, often with a costly gift on his person? As though in league with spirits, the robber band knew exactly when anything of this sort was taking place. Very often the unfortunate traveler never reached the house in which he hoped to enjoy the delights of love; very often he fell upon the threshold, or even outside the room of his mistress, who had the horrifying experience of finding his blood-stained corpse.

In vain did Argenson, the minister of police, have everyone arrested about whom there was the least suspicion. The king set up a special court for the exclusive purpose of investigating and punishing these crimes. This court was called the Chambre Ardente, which sat near the Bastille and was presided over by La Régnie. In vain La Régnie raged and tried to extort confessions; in vain were watches and patrols strengthened. No trace of the wrongdoers was to be found. The precaution of going armed to the teeth and preceded by a torchbearer helped, but only to a limited extent. Even then it sometimes happened that the servant was scared off by a hail of stones and the master murdered and robbed.

One morning Desgrais, of the Maréchaussée, came to President La Régnie in a state of agitation, his face pale and contorted.

"What news have you?" asked the president of the court. "Are you on their tracks?"

"Ha, Monsieur!" began Desgrais, enraged. "Last night—not far from the Louvre—the Marquis de la Fare was attacked in my presence. I was standing by the Louvre, watching out for these devils. A figure passed with faltering step, continually looking over his shoulder. He did not see me. In the moonlight I recognized the Marquis de la Fare. He was a bare ten or twelve paces from me when a figure sprang up as though from the earth, struck him down, and fell upon him. Without stopping to think, I let out a yell and sprang from my hiding place to assail him. In my haste I tripped over my cloak and fell headlong. I saw the man racing away as though on wings. I jumped to my feet and ran after him, blowing my horn as I did. Policemen's whistles answered me from the distance. Turmoil broke out. Weapons rattled and horses' hooves clattered on all sides.

"'Here! Here! Desgrais!' I cried, so that it echoed through the streets. We came to the Rue Nicaise. I strained my own strength to the utmost. He was no more than fifteen paces ahead of me—"

"You caught up with him! You seized him! The police arrived!" cried La Régnie with flashing eyes.

"Fifteen paces in front of me, the man jumped into the shadow at the side of the street and vanished through the wall."

"Vanished? Through the wall? Are you mad?"

"Call me mad. Tell me I suffer from hallucinations, but it was as I say. I was standing dumbfounded in front of the wall, when several policemen came panting up, accompanied by the Marquis de la Fare. We lit torches and tapped up and down the wall. Not a sign of a door, a window, or any opening. It was a solid stone wall enclosing a courtyard, and inside it was a house occupied by people entirely above suspicion. I made a careful examination of the place again today. It is the devil himself who is making fools of us."

Desgrais's story spread through Paris. Argenson petitioned the king to set up a court for the new crimes possessed of even wider powers than the Chambre Argente but the king dismissed the suggestion out of hand. Another means of stimulating the king to act was soon hit upon.

In the Marquise de Maintenon's apartment, where the King spent his afternoons, a poem was delivered in the name of "Endangered Lovers," complaining that while gallantry demanded that lovers should take their mistresses costly presents, it now meant risking their lives to woo their loves. While it was a joy and an honor to shed blood for their beloveds in knightly combat, it was quite a different matter to face the treacherous assault of murderers, against which there was no defense.

The Endangered Lovers called upon Louis, the shining polestar of all love and gallantry, to blaze forth and dissipate the darkness of night, uncovering the black mystery concealed with it. Let the divine hero now draw his victorious flashing sword again and strike down—as Hercules struck down the Lernean Hydra and Theseus the Minotaur—the fearful monster that was undermining all the pleasures of love and turning all joy into deep grief and inconsolable mourning.

The king turned to Maintenon, reading the poem through again, this time aloud, and asking with a charming smile what she thought of the "Endangered Lovers" and their pleas. Maintenon replied that secret and forbidden journeys did not deserve any special protection, but that the loathsome criminals certainly merited special measures for their extirpation.

The king walked toward Mlle de Scudéry, who sat in a small armchair close to the Marquise.

"The Marquise doesn't want to know about the gallantries of our enamored gentlemen and their perfectly legitimate activities and evades my question. But you, Mademoiselle, what do you think of this poetic petition?"

Mlle de Scudéry rose respectfully from her armchair, a fleeting flush like the red sunset passing across her cheeks, and curtseyed slightly:

> *"A lover, afraid of thieves,*
> *Is unworthy of love."*

The king, astonished by the chivalrous spirit of these few words encompassed in a striking couplet that made mincemeat of the poem of the "Endangered Lovers" cried with flashing eyes:

"By St. Denis, you are right, Mademoiselle! Cowardice shall not be protected by any blind measures that fall upon the innocent along with the guilty! Let Argenson and La Régnie do what they can!"

Martinière conjured up all the horrors of the night when she told her mistress next morning what had happened, and handed her the mysterious casket with fear and trembling. She and Baptiste, white-faced and almost speechless with dread, implored Mademoiselle to be careful in opening the casket.

Mlle de Scudéry smiled. "You are both seeing ghosts. The villainous assassins know as well as you or I that I am not rich and that there is no treasure here worth murdering for. You think my life is in danger? Who can have any interest in the death of a woman of seventy-three who has never persecuted anyone but the miscreants and ruffians in the novels she writes? who produces mediocre verse that can arouse no one's envy? who will leave nothing behind but the finery of an old spinster who occasionally goes to court? and a few dozen well-bound books with gilded edges? However terrible the description you give of the stranger, Martinière, I cannot believe that he intended evil. So what have we to fear?"

Martinière recoiled three paces. Baptiste sank half to his knees with a hollow groan. Mademoiselle now pressed a steel knob on the casket, causing the lid to spring open with a click.

A pair of gold bracelets set with jewels and a matching necklace sparkled up at her from the casket. She took out the jewelry, praising the superb workmanship of the necklace. Martinière eyed the costly bracelets.

"But what is this?" murmured Mlle de Scudéry, unfolding a sheet of paper at the bottom of the casket. Hardly had she read it than the note fell from her trembling hands. Then she turned her eyes to heaven and sank back in her armchair.

"The insult!" she cried in a voice half choked with tears. "The shame! Must I suffer such a thing at my time of life? Are words uttered without reflection and half in jest capable of such a horrifying interpretation? Are criminals to accuse me, a woman blameless and true to virtue and piety from childhood? Are criminals to accuse me of being in league with the devil?"

Martinière picked up the fateful message from the floor. It read:

"A lover, afraid of thieves,
Is unworthy of love.

"Your ready wit, Mademoiselle, has saved us—who exercise the right of the stronger upon the weak and cowardly and acquire valuables that would have been unworthily squandered—from great persecution. Please accept this jewelry as proof of our gratitude. It is the most costly we have been able to lay hands on for a long time, although you, worthy lady, should be adorned with far finer jewelry than this. We beg you not to withdraw from us your friendship and your gracious remembrance.

The Invisible Ones."

"Is it possible for shameless impudence and wicked mockery to be carried so far?" exclaimed Mlle de Scudéry when she had to some extent recovered from her shock.

The sun shone brightly through her red silk curtains, making the gems lying on the table beside the casket flash with a reddish gleam. Mlle de Scudéry covered her face with her hands and ordered Martinière to remove the frightful jewelry spattered with the blood of murdered men. Martinière suggested that the best thing to do would be to hand them over to the Minister of Police and tell him about the terrifying visitor of the night before.

The Marquise de Maintenon was surprised to see Mlle de Scudéry, generally the embodiment of dignity, enter her apartment that afternoon with tottering steps, her face pale and drawn.

"What in heaven's name has happened to you?"

Mlle de Scudéry, distraught, and barely able to stand upright, took the casket of jewelry to the armchair and sat down heavily. After a moment, she told of the deep and rankling insult brought upon her by the thoughtless jest with which she had answered the poetic petition of the Endangered Lovers.

The Marquise listened carefully, and then asked to see the gems. Mlle de Scudéry handed her the open casket. The Marquise could not restrain a loud exclamation of wonder at the sight of the costly ornaments. She took out the necklace and held it to the sunlight, next lifting the delicate gold work close to her eyes to study it more closely.

"Do you know, Mademoiselle, these bracelets and this necklace cannot have been made by anyone but René Cardillac!"

Cardillac was the most skilled goldsmith in Paris, and one of the most ingenious and singular men of his day. Below medium height, but broad-shouldered and of powerful, muscular build, Cardillac still possessed the strength and agility of a young man, although he was well into his fifties. He had thick, curly red hair, and a compact, shiny face. If he had not been known throughout Paris as an upright man of honor, the strange expression in his small, flashing green eyes might have suggested secret cunning and malignity.

The most skilled master of his craft in France, he knew how to treat and set gems in such a way that they left his shop in shining glory. He accepted every commission with burning eagerness, fixing a price so low as to be out of all proportion to the labor. Then, when the work was almost complete, he would take a sudden dislike to it and throw the whole ornament back into the melting pot to start in afresh.

As a result, everything he did emerged as a pure and insurpassable masterpiece that astonished his customers. But it was almost impossible to obtain any finished work from him. He would keep a customer waiting week after week, month after month. If, finally, he had to yield to the customer's pressure and hand over the jewelry, he could not conceal all the signs of profound chagrin and inward rage. If he had to deliver a piece of work of exceptional importance and value, perhaps worth several thousand louis by virtue of the costliness of the gems and the supreme delicacy of the goldsmith's work, he would often rampage as though distracted, cursing his work and everything around him.

For some inexplicable reason it sometimes happened that Cardillac, after accepting a commission with enthusiasm, would suddenly beg the customer to release him from the task he had undertaken. Many people highly esteemed by the king had vainly offered large sums for even the smallest piece of work by Cardillac. For one, he refused to accept any commission from the Marquise de Maintenon. Indeed, he rejected with every appearance of repugnance and horror her request to manufacture a small ring decorated with emblems of the arts, which she wished to present to the playwright Racine.

The Marquise exclaimed: "I wager that if I send for Cardillac to find out for whom he made these pieces of jewelry, he will refuse to come. He fears that I may wish to order something from him, and he is determined not to work for me."

Mlle de Scudéry suggested that the temperamental maestro might consent to come if they made it clear that they did not wish to commission work from him, but merely to consult him regarding certain gems. Cardillac was then sent for, and since the messenger found him in, it was not long before he entered the Marquise de Maintenon's room.

When he caught sight of Mlle de Scudéry he seemed disconcerted. He bowed deeply and reverently and only then turned to the Marquise. She pointed to the gems on the table and inquired if they were his work.

Cardillac hurriedly packed the necklace and bracelets in the casket, barely looking at them, and thrust it violently away from him. Smiling an ugly, almost sinister, smile, he said:

"Indeed, Madame la Marquise, you must be ill acquainted with my work if you can believe for a moment that any other goldsmith in the world could produce such articles. Of course it's my work!"

"Tell us for whom you made them," urged the Marquise.

"For no one but myself," replied Cardillac.

The Marquise and Mlle de Scudéry stared at him in astonishment, the former full of mistrust, the latter full of trepidation and apprehension.

"You may think it strange, Madame la Marquise, but that's how it is. For no other reason than to produce something really first class, I gathered together my finest gems and for the sheer joy of it worked on them more carefully and diligently than ever before. A short while ago, the pieces inexplicably disappeared from my workshop."

Mlle de Scudéry's eyes sparkled for joy. Quickly she jumped up from her armchair and strode across to Cardillac, placing both hands on his shoulders. "Master Cardillac, take back the property of which the rascally thieves have robbed you!" Then she related how the jewelry had come into her possession.

When she was done, Cardillac rubbed his forehead and ran his hand over his eyes. He seized the casket and held it out to her:

"Destiny intended these jewels for you, noble and worthy lady. I now realize for the first time that I was thinking of you while I was engaged upon them. Do not scorn to accept and wear this jewelry, the best I have made for a long time."

"What are you thinking of, Master René?" Mlle de Scudéry said jestingly. "If I were as beautiful as the Marquise de Fontange and rich, indeed I should not let these ornaments slip through my fingers. But what place is there for this vain splendor on these shriveled arms, for this glittering adornment around this wrinkled neck?"

Cardillac rose. "Have pity on me, Mademoiselle, and take the jewelry! You have no idea what veneration for your virtue and your high merits I carry in my heart!"

As Mlle de Scudéry hesitated, the Marquise de Maintenon took the casket from Cardillac. "Heavens above, Mademoiselle, you keep talking about your age. What have you and I to do with age and its burdens? Do not reject honest Master René, who is offering you as a present what thousands of others cannot get for all their gold and all their entreaties."

Cardillac fell to his knees, kissed Mlle de Scudéry's skirt, her hands, groaned, sighed, wept, sobbed, jumped up and ran madly from the room, knocking over chairs and tables in his blind haste.

Greatly startled, Mlle de Scudéry cried: "By all the saints, what's the matter with the man?"

The Marquise laughed. "Master René is desperately in love with you, and is beginning to assail your heart with costly gifts!" She even carried the jest further, admonishing Mlle de Scudéry not to be too cruel towards her despairing lover.

Mademoiselle, carried away by the torrent of witty fancies, commented that if things were really like that, she would present to the world the unique picture of a goldsmith's bride seventy-three years old and of unimpeachable nobility. Maintenon offered to weave the bridal wreath and to instruct her in the duties of a good housewife.

Despite the laughter and the jesting, Mlle de Scudéry once more became very serious as she finally rose to leave.

"I shall never be able to use this jewelry. It was once in the hands of those hellish ruffians who rob and murder Parisians with the impudence of the devil. I shudder to think of the blood that seems to adhere to this sparkling jewelry. Now even Cardillac's behavior appears to me strangely sinister and frightening. I cannot escape a dark foreboding that there is some hideous, horrifying secret behind all this."

The Marquise protested that this was carrying mistrust too far, but when asked what she would do in her place, the Marquise replied gravely:

"I would far rather throw the jewelry into the Seine than ever wear it."

Mlle de Scudéry's encounter with Master René led her to compose some delightful verses which she read out to the king next evening in Maintenon's apartment. She painted in vivid colors the amusing picture of the seventy-three year old goldsmith's bride of unimpeachable nobility. The king laughed heartily and the poem became regarded as the wittiest Mlle de Scudéry had ever written.

Several months later Mlle de Scudéry was driving over the Pont-Neuf in the Duchesse de Montausier's glass coach. The gaping rabble on the Pont-Neuf, crowding around to watch, almost brought the horses to a halt.

Suddenly a deathly pale and anguished young man, using his fists and elbows, forced his way through the densest mass of humanity toward the coach. He battled his way to the door of the coach, tore it open, and threw a note into Mlle de Scudéry's lap. Then he vanished as he had come.

Martinière, seated beside Mlle de Scudéry, uttered a cry of horror and fell back senseless against the cushions. The coachman whipped up the horses, which reared and struck out with their hooves, then thundered off across the bridge at a brisk trot.

Revived with smelling salts, Martinière groaned: "In the name of the Blessed Virgin, what did that terrible man want? It was he—yes, he!—who brought you the casket!"

Mlle de Scudéry unfolded the sheet of paper, which read:

"An evil fate, which you can avert, is thrusting me into the abyss! I beseech you, as a son addressing a mother to whom he is attached with all the ardor of childish love, return the necklace and bracelets you received from me to Master René Cardillac on some pretext or other—to have some improvement or alteration made, or something of that sort. Your welfare, your very life depends upon it. If you do not do so by the day after tomorrow, I shall force my way into your house and kill myself before your eyes!"

When she had read the letter, Mlle de Scudéry reasoned, "It is certain that even if the mysterious young man does belong to the band of villainous thieves and murderers, he has no evil intentions toward me. I shall do what I am bid in this note, if only to rid myself of the accursed jewelry, which seems like an unlucky charm that puts the possessor under a curse."

Social engagements prevented her from visiting Master René Cardillac that day. However, as soon as the sun was up the next morning she had herself dressed and set out in her carriage for the goldsmith's house, carrying the casket.

To her surprise, she saw that much of the populace was also streaming towards the Rue Nicaise, where Cardillac lived. In fact, they were gathering outside the door of his house. Yelling, clamoring, raging, and trying to break in, the rabble was held back by the mounted police, who had the house surrounded.

"Tear the accursed murderer limb from limb!" the crowd screamed. "Crush him!"

Finally Desgrais appeared with a number of his men, forming a passage through the mob. The door of the house sprang open and a man weighed down by chains was brought out and dragged off to the accompaniment of virulent curses from the mob. Mlle de Scudéry, almost swooning with shock and a terrible foreboding, heard a shrill cry of distress.

"Forward!" she cried to the coachman, who maneuvered through the mob up to Cardillac's front door. Here Desgrais stood, looking down at a lovely young girl—hair hanging loose, half naked, an expression of wild fear and hopeless despair on her face— embracing his knees and crying out in tones of heart-rending anguish:

"He is innocent!"

In vain did Desgrais and his men strive to lift her from the ground and pull her away. Finally an uncouth, muscular fellow took hold her arms and dragged her away by sheer force. She fell from him and lay in the street without a sound as if dead.

Mlle de Scudéry opened the coach door and stepped out. "In the name of Christ, what has happened? What is going on?" The crowd made way for her as she picked up the girl and placed her on the stone steps.

Desgrais approached. "Something terrible," he said. "René Cardillac was found stabbed to death this morning. His apprentice,

Olivier Brusson, is the murderer. He has just been taken off to prison."

"And the girl?"

"Is Madelon, Cardillac's daughter," Desgrais explained. "The murderer was her lover. Now she weeps and wails and cries over and over again that he is innocent. In the end I shall probably find that she knew all about the deed and shall have to take her to the Conciergerie as well." The Conciergerie was Paris's central prison.

The girl was regaining consciousness, but lay there with her eyes still closed. Mlle de Scudéry quickly made up her mind. "I shall take her with me," she told Desgrais. "You can see to the rest!"

A murmur of approval ran through the crowd, and as Mlle de Scudéry lifted Madelon up, a hundred hands came to her aid.

After hours of rest and attendance by a physician, Madelon was finally able to speak, and she told Mlle de Scudéry what had happened. Awakened around midnight by a knocking at her door, she heard her lover Olivier's voice beseeching her to rise because her father was dying. In horror she had jumped up to accompany him.

Olivier, his face pale and contorted, dripping with sweat, and carrying a light, had made his way to the workshop. There she found her father lying with staring eyes, his shirt stained with blood, his throat rattling as he struggled with death.

Drawing her gently away, Olivier tended a chest wound on her father's left side, washing it with balm and bandaging it. Her father recovered his senses, gave Madelon a look of deep feeling, took her hand, placed it in Olivier's, and pressed their two hands passionately. They fell to their knees at his bedside. Cardillac then sat up with a piercing cry, sank back, and with a deep sigh, died.

Olivier told Madelon that at his master's request he had gone for a walk with him during the night, that Cardillac had been murdered in his presence, and that Olivier had carried the big, heavy man home with the greatest difficulty, not believing him mortally wounded.

At daybreak an uproar had broken out when the other occupants of the house had come upstairs and found them kneeling in despair beside her father's corpse. The Maréchaussée had forced their way in and dragged Olivier off to prison as his master's murderer.

Madelon now added the most moving description of the virtue, piety, and fidelity of her beloved Olivier: how he had honored his master; how the latter had returned his love; how despite his poverty Cardillac had chosen him as his son-in-law. Madelon declared that if Olivier had thrust the dagger into her father's breast in her presence she would have taken it for a satanic hallucination rather than have believed him capable of such a crime.

Profoundly moved by Madelon's unspeakable suffering and fully prepared to believe poor Olivier guiltless, Mlle de Scudéry made inquiries and found all Madelon's statements regarding the domestic relations between the master and his apprentice confirmed. The other occupants of the house unanimously praised Olivier as a model of virtuous, devout, true, and industrious behavior. No one had a bad word to say against him. When the abominable deed was spoken of, they shrugged their shoulders and commented that there was some mystery there.

Before the Chambre Ardente Olivier denied the murder with steadfastness and candor, asserting that his master had been attacked in his presence in the street and struck down, and that Olivier had carried him still alive to his home, where Cardillac had died. This, too, tallied with Madelon's account.

After investigating all the circumstances on the assumption that, in spite of everything that spoke so loudly for his innocence, Olivier nevertheless was Cardillac's murderer, Mlle de Scudéry was unable to imagine any possible motive for the terrible deed.

"He is poor, but skillful," she decided. "He succeeded in gaining the affection of the most famous of all master goldsmiths. He loves the daughter. The master approved of him. Lifelong happiness and prosperity awaited him. If Olivier actually made a murderous assault upon his benefactor, what demonic hypocrisy it would have required to act as in fact he did act!"

Firmly convinced of Olivier's innocence, Mlle de Scudéry resolved to save the innocent youth, cost what it might. She felt it would be best to approach President La Régnie, draw his attention to all the facts that spoke in Olivier's favor, and perhaps arouse in him an inner conviction of the suspect's innocence which he might communicate to the judges of the court.

La Régnie received Mlle de Scudéry with the proper deference of a worthy lady who was held in high honor by the king himself. He listened quietly to everything she had to say about the horrible deed and about Olivier's life and character. A subtle, almost malicious smile was the only sign that her protestations and her counsel had fallen on totally deaf ears.

"It does credit to your kind heart, Mademoiselle," La Régnie said when she had finished, "that you believe all a young girl in love tells you, in fact that you find the horrifying crime altogether incomprehensible. It is different for a judge, who is accustomed to tearing away the mask of impudent hypocrisy from the guilty. But I do not wish to be considered a monster of harshness and cruelty. Therefore let me conclusively prove to you the blood guilt of the young scoundrel Brusson.

"In the morning René Cardillac was found stabbed to death, nobody was with him but the apprentice Olivier Brusson and his daughter. In Olivier's room was found, among other things, a dagger smeared with fresh blood that exactly fitted the wound.

"'Cardillac,' Olivier testified, 'was struck down in the street before my eyes during the night.'

"'Did the murderer intend to rob him?'

"'I do not know.'

"'You were walking with him. Couldn't you have warded off the murderer? Couldn't you have caught hold of him? Couldn't you have called for help?'

"'The master was walking fifteen, probably twenty paces, in front of me. I was following him.'

"'Why were you so far from him?'

"'The master wished it so.'

"'Why was Master Cardillac out in the street so late at night?'

"'I cannot say.'

"'But ordinarily he never went out of the house after nine in the evening, did he?'

"At this point, Olivier hesitated. He was perplexed. He sighed. He shed tears. He protested by everything holy that Cardillac really did go out that night and met his death in the street. But take careful notice, Mademoiselle. It has been proved with absolute certainty to me that Cardillac *never left the house that night*. Hence Olivier's assertion that he went out with him is an impudent lie.

"The front door of the house is fitted with a heavy lock that makes a piercing noise when it is opened and shut. Also, the door makes a terrible grinding and screeching as it moves on its hinges, a din which, as experiments have proved, reaches even to the top of the house.

"Now on the ground floor—that is to say, next to the door—old Master Claude Patru lives with his housekeeper, a woman close on eighty, but still bright and nimble.

"These two people heard Cardillac come downstairs as usual that evening on the stroke of nine, lock and bolt the door, then mount the stairs again, read out the evening prayer aloud, and then, as could be heard from the banging of the doors, go into his bedroom.

"Like many old people, Master Claude suffers from insomnia. That night he never closed his eyes. At about ten o'clock, the housekeeper crossed the entrance hall into the kitchen, put on the light, and sat down with Master Claude at the table and read, while the old man mused, now in the armchair, now walking slowly to and fro in search of sleep.

"Everything was quiet till after midnight. Then they heard vigorous footsteps overhead, a hard bump, as though a heavy object was falling to the floor, and immediately afterwards a muffled groaning. Both were filled with a strange fear and dread. The horror of the atrocious deed that had just been committed simply passed over them without arousing their suspicions. When day broke, the light revealed what had been done in the dark."

"But in the name of all the saints," Mlle de Scudéry broke in, "after all I have told you, can you imagine any motive for this hellish deed?"

"Cardillac was not poor," replied La Régnie. "He possessed some splendid gems."

"But was it not all going to the daughter?" Mlle de Scudéry continued. "You forget that Olivier was to become Cardillac's son-in-law."

"Perhaps he had to share the spoils with others," said La Régnie. "Olivier is evidently a member of that villainous band that has carried out its misdeeds with impunity in spite of all the efforts of the law. Cardillac's wound is identical with the wounds sustained by all those who were murdered and robbed in the streets and in the houses. There is also a decisive fact that since the day of Olivier Brusson's arrest all murders and robberies have ceased. The streets are as safe at night as they are during the day!"

"And what about Madelon?" cried Mlle de Scudéry. "What about Madelon, the true, innocent dove?"

"As for her," said La Régnie with a venomous smile, "who will guarantee that she was not in the plot? What does she care about her father? All her tears are for the assassin."

"What are you saying? It is impossible! Her father—that girl?"

"You must forgive me if soon I find myself compelled to tear your protégée away from you and have her thrown into the Conciergerie."

A shudder ran through Mlle de Scudéry. She stood up. "Be humane!" she begged. She was about to descend the stairs when she was struck by a thought. "Should I be allowed to see the unhappy Olivier Brusson?"

La Régnie looked at her thoughtfully, his face twisted into his characteristic repellent smile. "If you do not shrink from the gloomy abode of crime, if it is not repugnant to you to see images of every gradation of depravity, the gates of the Conciergerie shall be opened to you in two hours' time."

On her arrival at the Conciergerie, Mlle de Scudéry was taken into a large, light room. Not long afterwards she heard the clanking of chains and Olivier Brusson was brought in. The moment he appeared in the doorway, Mlle de Scudéry looked into his face and sank to the floor in a swoon.

Olivier Brusson was the young man who had thrown the note into her carriage on the Pont-Neuf, the man who had brought her the casket containing the jewels! All doubt was now removed from her mind. La Régnie's dreadful supposition was fully confirmed. Olivier Brusson *was* a member of the gang of murderers. Without a doubt he had murdered his master.

Mlle de Scudéry demanded to be taken to her carriage, to leave at once the haunt of shameless villainy.

But what of Madelon? she wondered as she drove home. Could Madelon be in the plot herself, sharing the atrocious blood guilt of her lover?

As Mlle de Scudéry dismounted her carriage and entered her room, Madelon appeared and threw herself at her feet. Looking up with heavenly eyes, as pure as any angel of God, her hands folded over her heaving bosom, she wailed and loudly implored help and comfort.

Taking a grip on herself and seeking to give her voice as much gravity and calm as she could, Mlle de Scudéry said:

"Go! Go! Rejoice that a just punishment for his shameful deed awaits the murderer of your father. The Holy Virgin grant that no burden of blood guilt rests upon you yourself!"

"Oh, now all is lost!" Madelon fell senseless to the floor.

Mlle de Scudéry left Martinière to see to the girl and hurried into another room. She could hear Madelon's soft words as Martiniére led her out:

"Oh, she too—she too!—the cruel ones have deceived. Oh, wretched me! Oh, poor, unhappy Olivier!"

Distracted by the contradictory emotions of despair and justification, she sighed: "What spirit of hell has entangled me in this hideous affair that will cost me my reason?"

At that moment a pale and terrified Baptiste entered with the news that Desgrais was waiting outside. Since the recent reign of terror in Paris the appearance of Desgrais in any house had been the certain harbinger of some dreadful accusation; hence Baptiste's terror.

Mademoiselle smiled gently. "What's the matter with you, Baptiste?"

Trembling from head to foot, Baptiste replied: "Desgrais, the terrible Desgrais, is acting so mysteriously, with such urgency. It seems he simply can't wait to see you!"

"Bring in this man of whom you are so afraid, but who doesn't frighten me in the least."

"I have been sent by President La Régnie, Mademoiselle," said Desgrais once he was in the room. "Since seeing you, Olivier Brusson has become half demented. Whereas previously he seemed much disposed to confess, he now swears by Christ and all the saints that he is completely innocent of Cardillac's murder. Yet he desires to suffer the death he has deserved. This last remark obviously indicates that he is guilty of other crimes. Yet all efforts to drag another word from him have been in vain; even the threat of torture has proved fruitless. He entreats us to arrange for him to talk to you. To you, and to you alone, will he confess everything. Condescend, Mademoiselle, to hear Brusson's confession."

"I wish to know nothing of his secrets," Mlle de Scudéry said. "They would remain locked in my breast like a holy confession."

Desgrais smiled faintly. "You may change your mind when you

have heard Brusson. Did you not bid the President himself to be humane? He is doing so, by acceding to Brusson's fantastic request."

Mlle de Scudéry involuntarily winced.

"No one expects you to return to those gloomy chambers that filled you with horror and repugnance. Under cover of darkness, Olivier Brusson will be brought to you here. With none to overhear, he may confess everything of his own free will. He speaks of you with fervent veneration. He swears that only the grim fate which prevented him from seeing you sooner is hurling him to his death."

Mlle de Scudéry stood in profound reflection, realizing she could no longer escape the supernatural toils in which she had been involuntarily caught up. Making up her mind, she spoke with dignity:

"God will give me composure and fortitude. Bring Brusson here. I shall speak to him."

That midnight the door of her room opened quietly. Desgrais entered. Behind him stood Olivier Brusson, free from chains and decently dressed. Desgrais bowed and left the room. Brusson sank to his knees before Mlle de Scudéry and raised his folded hands imploringly, tears streaming from his eyes.

Mlle de Scudéry looked down at him, pale-faced and incapable of speech. His features radiated true goodness. The longer she looked at him, the more vivid was her recollection of someone she had loved, but whom she could not clearly identify.

"Well, Brusson," she said, "what have you to say to me?"

Kneeling, Brusson sighed profoundly. "Oh, noble lady, has all memory of me flown? Have you entirely forgotten Anne Guiot? It is her son, Olivier, whom you often dandled on your knee, who now stands before you."

Mlle de Scudéry covered her face with her hands and sank back into the cushions. "In the name of all the saints!" Anne Guiot, the daughter of an impoverished burgher, had lived from an early age with Mlle de Scudéry, who brought the dear child up with all a mother's loving care. As Anne grew up, she was wooed by a handsome, virtuous youth named Claude Brusson. Since he was a highly skilled clockmaker who earned a good living in Paris, and Anne had fallen in love with him, Mlle de Scudéry had no hesitation in consenting to her foster-daughter's marriage. The young couple lived in quiet happy domesticity, and the bond of love was tied yet tighter by the birth of a beautiful boy, the image of his lovely mother.

Mlle de Scudéry idolized little Olivier, as a result of which the boy grew attached to her and was as happy to be with her as with his mother. The little family moved three years later to Geneva, Brusson's lovely home town. Anne wrote to her foster-mother a few times, then she fell silent, and Mlle de Scudéry could only suppose that her happy life in Brusson's homeland had wiped out the memory of the past. It was now twenty-three years since the Brussons had left Paris for Geneva.

"Oh, horror," cried Mlle de Scudéry. "Are you Olivier? My Anne's son! To find you like this!"

"I am not blameless. The Chambre Ardente can justly charge me with a crime. But I am innocent of all blood guilt. It was not through me, not through my fault, that the unhappy Cardillac died."

Mlle de Scudéry silently motioned Olivier to a small armchair. Slowly he sat down.

"If only my poor father had never left Paris!" Olivier began. "My earliest memory of Geneva is of being sprinkled with the tears of my disconsolate parents and brought to tears myself by their laments. Later came the full consciousness of the oppressive want and profound poverty in which we lived. My father found himself disappointed in all his hopes. He died at the moment he succeeded in apprenticing me to a goldsmith.

"My mother spoke a great deal of you. She wanted to acquaint you with her sufferings, but she was overwhelmed by the discouragement born of her poverty. A few months after my father's death, she followed him into the grave.

"As for me, I was treated harshly by my master, although I worked hard and finally far outdid him. One day a foreigner happened to come into our workshop to buy some jewelry. Seeing a fine necklace I had made, he gave me a friendly slap on the back, eyed the ornament, and said:

"'Well, well, my young friend, this is an excellent piece of work. I really don't know who can surpass you except René Cardillac, who is the finest goldsmith in the world. You should go to him.'

"In the end I managed to break free from my master and came to Paris. René Cardillac received me coldly and gruffly. I refused to be put off. He told me to make a small ring. When I brought him the work he stared at me with his glittering eyes as though trying to see right inside me.

"'You are a first-rate craftsman. You can move in with me and help me in the workshop. I shall pay you well. You will be happy with me.'

"Cardillac kept his word. I had been with him for several weeks without seeing Madelon, who was staying in the country with a cousin. At last she returned. Oh, eternal power of heaven, what happened to me when I saw the angelic creature! Has anyone ever loved as I do? And now! Oh, Madelon!'"

Olivier's sorrow overcame him. He put both hands over his face and sobbed violently. Then, mastering himself finally, he continued:

"Madelon looked at me with friendly eyes. She came to the workshop more and more frequently. I perceived with delight that she loved me. Cardillac seemed not to notice anything. I planned to ask him for Madelon's hand. But one morning he came up to me with anger and contempt in his eyes.

"'I need your labor no longer. Out of this house within the hour. Let me never set eyes on you again. The sweet fruit after which you aspire hangs too high for you!' He seized me with his powerful hands and flung me out the door.

"I made my way to a kindly acquaintance who took me into his garret. I had no peace, no rest. At night I prowled round Cardillac's house, fancying that Madelon might be able to speak to me from the window.

"Next to Cardillac's house there is a high wall containing blind niches and old, half-crumbled statues. I was standing close beside one of these statues one night, looking up at the windows of the house when I saw a light in Cardillac's workshop. It was midnight. Cardillac was never awake at this hour; he habitually went to bed on the stroke of nine. The light immediately disappeared.

"I pressed myself against the statue and into the niche, but recoiled in horror when I felt a counter-pressure, as though the statue had come to life. In the gray dusk I then saw the statue slowly rotate and a dark figure slip out and make off down the street with soft footsteps. I sprang to the statue. It was once more standing close against the wall. I ran after the figure. The full light of the bright street lamp burning in front of the statue fell upon its face. It was Cardillac!

"An inexplicable fear, an eerie shudder, came over me. As though under a spell, I set out in pursuit of the ghostly somnambulist—for such I took the master to be, although it was not the time of the full moon, which thus bewitches sleepers. Cardillac vanished into the deep shadows beside him. I realized he had gone into the entryway of a house.

"It wasn't long before a man wearing a plumed hat and spurs came out of the house singing. Like a tiger upon his prey, Cardillac sprang from his place of concealment upon the man, who sank to the ground instantly, rattling in his throat. With a cry of horror, I leaped forward. Cardillac was bending over the man.

"'Master Cardillac, what are you doing?' I shouted.

"Cardillac recognized me. 'Curses on you!' he bellowed, and ran past me and disappeared. Quite beside myself and scarcely capable of moving a step, I approached the fallen man. I knelt down beside him. There was not a trace of life in him. In my anguish, I barely noticed that I had been surrounded by the Maréchaussée.

"'Another one laid low by the devils! Hey, young man, what are you doing here? Are you one of the gang? Away with you!'

"Someone shone a light into my face and laughed. 'That's Olivier Brusson, who works with our good, honest Master René Cardillac! He's very likely to murder people in the street—he's just the type! And then you'd expect a murderer to stay, lamenting by the corpse to let himself be caught. Come on, lad, tell us what happened.'

"'Just in front of me,' I told them, 'a man fell upon this one here, struck him down, and ran away as fast as lightning when I shouted. I was looking to see whether there was still a chance of saving him.'

"'No, my son,' exclaimed one. 'He's dead, stabbed through the heart as usual.'

"'Damnation,' said another. 'We've come too late again, like the day before yesterday.' With this they left, carrying the corpse.

"I cannot describe how I felt. Cardillac—the father of my Madelon—a villainous murderer! I returned to my garret and was sitting there completely bewildered when the door opened. René Cardillac came towards me, smiling with calm and serenity, and pulled up a rickety old stool.

"'Well, Olivier,' he began, 'how are you, poor lad? I was really terribly over-hasty when I threw you out of the house. How would it be if you came and worked with me again? I was angry about your flirtation with Madelon, but I thought things over and concluded that I couldn't wish a better son-in-law than you. So come with me and see if you can win Madelon for your wife.'

"I couldn't utter a word. He bored into me with his glittering eyes. 'Perhaps you want to pay a visit to Desgrais or even call upon Argenson or La Régnie. Take care, boy, that the claws which you wish to draw out to other people's destruction do not seize and tear you yourself!'

"'Let him who has a hideous crime on his conscience tremble at the names you have just uttered!' I cried. 'I have no need to. I have nothing to fear from them.'

"'As a matter of fact,' Cardillac continued, 'it would do you honor to work with me. I am the most famous master goldsmith of the day and esteemed everywhere for my honesty and straightforwardness. Any evil slander would fall back heavily upon the head of the slanderer. Madelon loves you with a vehemence with which I would not have credited the gentle child. Yesterday evening I told her that I consented to everything and would fetch you today. She blossomed out overnight like a rose and is now waiting for you.'

"May the eternal power of heaven forgive me, I don't know myself how it happened, but suddenly I was standing in Cardillac's house, and Madelon, crying exultantly, 'Olivier, my Olivier, my beloved, my husband!' rushed to me, threw her arms round my neck, and pressed herself to my breast. In the excess of joy I swore by the Holy Virgin and all the saints that I would never, never leave her."

Overwhelmed by his recollections, Olivier now fell silent. Mlle de Scudéry, horrified at the crime of a man whom she regarded as the embodiment of virtue and probity, exclaimed:

"It's terrible! René Cardillac is a member of the gang of murderers that has for so long turned our good city into a den of thieves?"

"Gang, Mademoiselle?" Olivier repeated. "There never was any gang. It was Cardillac *alone* who villainously sought and found his victims throughout the city. Because he was *alone* he was able to carry out his misdeeds with impunity. But let me continue. The sequel will reveal the secrets of the most villainous, and at the same time unhappiest, of men.

"When I worked with the old man in the workshop I could not look him in the face, could scarcely exchange a word with him.

Madelon, the pure, angelic child, idolized him. It cut me to the quick to think that if vengeance fell upon the unmasked villain, she, who had been deceived with all the hellish cunning of Satan, would be plunged into the most abysmal despair.

"One day Cardillac, who, to my intense disgust, generally used to be very gay while at work, turned extremely serious and withdrawn. He flung aside the piece of jewelry he was working on, scattering gems and pearls in all directions, jumped to his feet, and said:

"'Olivier, things cannot remain like this between us. The situation is unbearable. What the subtlest cunning of Desgrais and his henchmen failed to discover has been delivered into your hands by chance. Yet in your present position, betrayal is out of the question. You shall know all.'"

"He sat down on his working chair, wiping the sweat from his brow. He seemed profoundly shaken. He began: 'Wise men have a great deal to say about the strange impressions to which pregnant women are susceptible, about the curious influences they may exercise upon the child. An extraordinary story was told me of my mother. During the first month of pregnancy she watched, with other women, a magnificent court festival at Trianon. She caught sight of a cavalier in Spanish dress with a flashing jewelled necklace, from which she thereafter could not take her eyes. Her whole being became a desire for the sparkling gems, which appeared to her of supernatural worth.

"'Several years earlier, when my mother was not yet married, the same cavalier had made an attempt upon her virtue, but had been rejected with scorn. The cavalier observed my mother's yearning, fiery gaze. He believed that he would be luckier now than before. He approached her and lured her away from her acquaintances to a lonely spot. There he took her passionately in his arms. My mother grabbed at the beautiful necklace. The same instant he fell to the ground, dragging my mother down with him. Either because he had suffered a sudden stroke or for some other reason, he was dead.

"'My mother sought in vain to extricate herself from his rigid arms. Her shrill screams for help finally reached some people passing in the distance. They released her from the arms of her horrible lover. The shock made my mother seriously ill. She and I were given up for lost. But she recovered, and the birth was easier than anyone had hoped. But the terror of that frightful moment had struck me. My evil star had risen and shot down sparks that ignited in me a strange and ruinous passion.

"'Even in my earliest childhood I prized sparkling diamonds and the work of the goldsmith above everything. As a boy I stole gold and gems wherever I could lay my hands on them. Instinctively I distinguished fake jewelry from genuine. Only the genuine attracted me; fake gems and rolled gold I ignored.

"'In order to handle gold and precious stones I embraced the goldsmith's profession, soon becoming the leading master in this art. My inborn impulse, so long suppressed, forced its way to the surface. As soon as I had completed and delivered a piece of jewelry, I lapsed into a state of unrest and despair that robbed me of sleep, health, and the will to live. The person for whom I had worked stood day and night before my eyes, decked out in my jewelry, and a voice whispered in my ear: "It's yours—it's yours—take it—what use are diamonds to a dead man?"

"'In the end I began to steal. I had entrée into the houses of the great. I quickly made use of every opportunity. No lock resisted my skill. Soon the jewelry I had made was back in my hands. But even that did not dispel my restlessness. I began to feel unutterable hatred towards those for whom I made jewelry. An impulse to murder them began to stir in the depths of my soul, at which I myself trembled.

"'It was then that I bought this house. I had come to terms with the seller, we were sitting together in this room, drinking a bottle of wine to celebrate. I was about to leave, when he said: Listen, Master René, before you go I must acquaint you with a secret of this house." So saying, he opened a cupboard built into the wall, pushed the back of the cupboard aside, stepped through into a small closet, bent down, and raised a trap door. We went down a steep and narrow flight of stairs, came to a narrow gate, which he opened, and emerged into the courtyard.

"'Now the old gentleman walked across to the encircling wall, pushed at a slightly projecting piece of iron, and immediately part of the wall revolved, so that a man could comfortably step through the opening and out into the street. The device was probably made by cunning monks of the monestary that once stood here, so that they could secretly slip in and out. It is a piece of wood, mortared and whitewashed on the outside, into which a statue, also of wood, has been let; wall and statue together rotate on hidden hinges.

"'Dark thoughts rose in me as I looked at this device. It seemed foreshadowing for deeds which as yet remained a secret even to myself. I had just delivered to a gentleman of the Court a rich ornament which was intended for a dancer at the opera. I was subjected to terrible torments; the ghost dogged my footsteps.

"'I moved into the house. Bathed in the sweat of terror, I tossed and turned sleepless on my bed. I could see the man slipping off to the dancer with my jewelry. Furious, I jumped up, threw on my coat, went down the secret stairs, and out through the wall into the Rue Nicaise. He came. I fell upon him. He shouted. I held him fast from behind and plunged my dagger into his heart. The jewelry was mine!

"'This done, I felt such calm, such contentment in my soul as I had never known before. The ghost was gone, the voice of Satan silent. Now I knew what my evil star desired. I had to obey or perish!'

"Having said all this, Cardillac led me into the secret vault and let me look at his jewel cabinet. The king himself does not own a finer one. Attached to each article was a small label stating exactly for whom it was made and when it was taken by theft, robbery, or violence.

"'On your wedding day, Olivier,' said Cardillac in a hollow, solemn voice, 'you will swear a sacred oath with your hand on the crucifix that as soon as I am dead you will reduce all these riches to dust by means with which I shall acquaint you. I do not want any human being, and least of all Madelon and you, to come into possession of this hoard bought with blood.'

"Caught in this maze of crime, torn by love and repugnance, by bliss and horror, I was like a damned soul whom a lovely angel, gently smiling, beckons up aloft, while Satan holds him fast with red-hot claws. I thought of flight, even of suicide—but I could not leave Madelon!

"One day Cardillac came home unusually gay. He fondled Madelon, gave me a most friendly look, drank a bottle of vintage wine at supper, sang, and exulted. Madelon had left us and I was about to go into the workshop.

"'Sit where you are, lad,' cried Cardillac. 'No more work today. Let us drink to the welfare of the worthiest and most excellent lady in Paris.'

"After I had clinked glasses with him and he had drained his at a gulp, he said: 'Tell me, Olivier, how do you like these lines: *"A lover, afraid of thieves, Is unworthy of love"?'*

"He then told me what had happened in the Marquise de Maintenon's apartment between yourself and the king, adding that he had always revered you above every human being and that you, with your lofty virtue, would never arouse any evil spirit, any thoughts of murder, in him, even if you were to put on the finest jewelry he had ever made.

"'Listen, Olivier,' he said. 'A long time ago I was commissioned to make a necklace and bracelet for Henrietta of England and to supply the gems myself. You know of the Princess's unhappy death by assassination. I kept the jewelry and wish now, as a token of my veneration and gratitude, to send it to Mlle de Scudéry in the name of the persecuted band. Besides, if I deliver to Mlle de Scudéry this token of her triumph, I shall also be pouring upon Desgrais and his fellows the scorn they merit. You shall take the jewelry to her.'

"As soon as Cardillac spoke your name, Mademoiselle, it was as though black veils had been torn aside and the beautiful, bright picture of my happy early childhood rose before me in gay and shining colors. A wonderful feeling of consolation entered my heart, a ray of hope before which the gloomy spirits vanished.

"'You seem to be pleased with my plan,' he said. He then told me exactly how and when I was to deliver the jewelry, which he enclosed in an elegant casket. I was filled with delight, for, completely against Cardillac's wishes, I intended to insist upon seeing you personally. As Anne Brusson's son and your foster-child, I meant to throw myself at your feet and tell you everything. Your brilliant mind would have been able to devise some means of controlling his abominable wickedness without revealing it. The conviction that you would save Madelon and me was deeply implanted in my soul as my faith in the help and comfort of the Holy Virgin.

"You know, Mademoiselle, that my plan miscarried that night. Cardillac lost all his gaiety. He crept gloomily around, staring into space and muttering unintelligibly and striking the air with his hands. I saw your life threatened by his desire for the gems. I reasoned that if Cardillac only had his jewelry in his possession again, you would be saved. I met you on the Pont-Neuf and threw you a note imploring you to bring back to Cardillac the jewelry you had received from him. You did not come. Cardillac spoke of nothing else than the costly jewelry. I was certain that he was brooding upon a murderous assault.

"As soon as he had shut himself in his room after evening prayers, I climbed out of a window into the courtyard, slipped through the opening in the wall, and took up a position close by in deep shadow. I followed him when he came out. He went toward the Rue Saint-Honoré. All of a sudden I lost sight of him. I resolved to station myself at your front door to protect you. An officer passed, singing, without noticing me. At the same moment a black figure leapt out and fell upon him. It was Cardillac.

"I uttered a loud cry. In two or three bounds I was on the spot. It was not the officer, but Cardillac, who sank to the ground mortally wounded, and with the death rattle in his throat. The officer dropped the dagger, drew his sword from its sheath. Thinking I was the murderer's accomplice, he took up a fighting stance. When he saw that I paid no attention to him, but simply examined the corpse, he hurried quickly away. Cardillac was still alive. After picking up the dagger which the officer had dropped, I hoisted Cardillac onto my shoulders and with an effort carried him home and through the secret passage to the workshop.

"The rest you know."

Olivier fell silent, a river of tears gushed from his eyes, and he threw himself at Mlle de Scudéry's feet. "Have pity on me! Tell me how Madelon is."

A few minutes later Madelon flung herself on his breast. "Everything is all right, now that you are here. I knew the noble-hearted lady would save you!" cried Madelon.

The bright rays of morning were breaking through the window. Desgrais knocked softly on the door, and reminded those within that it was time to take Olivier Brusson away.

Mlle de Scudéry now saw the son of her beloved Anne innocent, but so entangled by circumstances that there seemed no way to save him from a shameful death. She honored the young man's heroism, which made him prefer to die laden with apparent guilt rather than reveal a secret that would cause Madelon's death.

She could think of no possible means of snatching the poor fellow from the Court, and yet she was determined to shun no sacrifice which might avert the crying injustice that was in the process of being committed.

Mlle de Scudéry wrote a long letter to La Régnie telling him that Olivier Brusson had proved to her complete satisfaction that he had no hand in Cardillac's death, and that only a heroic resolve to take with him to the grave a secret whose revelation would bring ruin upon true innocence and virtue prevented him from making a statement to the Court that would free him.

A few hours after receiving the letter, La Régnie replied that he was sincerely delighted to hear that Brusson had convinced his exalted and worthy patroness of his innocence. However, he was sorry that the Chambre Ardente could not honor such heroism, but must rather seek to break it by the most forceful means.

Mlle de Scudéry knew only too well what the terrible La Régnie meant by breaking Brusson's silence: he meant torture. Mlle de Scudéry immediately sought the advice of a lawyer, Pierre Arnauld D'Andilly, the most famous advocate in Paris.

She told him everything. D'Andilly listened and then replied, smiling, with Boileau's words: "Truth may sometimes look improbable." He pointed out that there was the strongest evidence against Brusson, that La Régnie's procedure could in no way be called brutal or hasty, that he was entirely within the law, and in fact could not act in any other way without neglecting his duty.

"Then I shall throw myself at the king's feet and beg for his mercy," said Mlle de Scudéry.

"For heaven's sake don't do that, Mademoiselle," urged D'Andilly. "Reserve that measure as a last resort! It is possible that by revealing his secret or by some other means, Brusson will succeed in exculpating himself in the eyes of the law."

Mlle de Scudéry had no alternative but to take D'Andilly's advice. She was sitting late that evening in her room when Martinière entered and announced Count Miossens, a colonel in the King's Guard, who urgently wished to speak to Mademoiselle.

After bowing with soldierly decorum, Miossens spoke. "Forgive me, Mademoiselle, for intruding upon you so late. I am here on account of Olivier Brusson."

"What have you to do with him?"

"The whole world is convinced of Brusson's guilt. No one can be more convinced than I am that Brusson had no hand in Cardillac's death. It was I who struck down the old goldsmith in the Rue Saint-Honoré."

"By all the saints—you?" cried Mlle de Scudéry.

"And I swear to you, Mademoiselle, that I am proud of my deed. Know that Cardillac was the most abominable and hypocritical villain, that it was he who cunningly murdered and robbed by night and for so long escaped every snare. I do not know myself what aroused my suspicions of the old villain, when, in a state of visible unrest, he brought me the jewelry I had ordered, inquired in detail for whom it was intended, and in the craftiest manner questioned my valet as to when I was in the habit of visiting a certain lady.

"It had long since struck me that the unfortunate victims of this loathsome robber all bore the same fatal wound. I realized that the murderer had practiced a particular blow which must kill instantly, and that he counted on it. If he missed, it meant a fight. I therefore took a precaution which is so simple I am amazed that others did not think of it before. I wore a light breastplate under my waistcoat.

"Cardillac attacked me from behind. He gripped me with the strength of a giant, but his deadly accurate blow slipped off the iron. The same instant I broke free from his grasp and stabbed him in the chest with the dagger I held ready."

"And you are silent?" mused Mlle de Scudéry. "You do not make a statement to the court?"

"Such a statement, if it did not ruin me, might at least involve me in the most repugnant trial. Would La Régnie, who scents crime everywhere, believe me if I accused the honest Cardillac, the model of piety and virtue, of murder? Suppose the sword of justice were pointed at me?"

"But in this way you will bring the innocent Brusson to the scaffold!"

"If I have told you the true facts of the case, Mademoiselle, it was on the understanding that you would know how to use my secret for the benefit of your protégé without delivering me into the hands of the Chambre Ardente."

Overjoyed to find her conviction of Brusson's innocence so decisively confirmed, Mlle de Scudéry had no hesitation in revealing everything to the Count, since he already knew of Cardillac's crimes. She asked him to go with her to D'Andilly to tell him the whole story.

D'Andilly asked Count Miossens if he was certain that he had been attacked by Cardillac and if he would be able to identify Olivier Brusson as the person who had carried away the corpse.

"I clearly recognized the goldsmith in the moonlit night," replied Miossens. "I also saw in La Régnie's possession the dagger with which Cardillac was stabbed. It is mine. I was standing only a pace from the young man, whose hat had fallen from his head, and could see his every feature. I should have no difficulty in identifying him."

D'Andilly stared into space a moment. "Even if Brusson proved this accusation by revealing the secret panel in the wall and the hoard of stolen jewelry, he would still be condemned to death as an accomplice of Cardillac. The same holds true if Miossens were to reveal to the judges what really happened to the goldsmith. Delay is all we can hope to achieve for the present. Let Miossens call at the Conciergerie, have Brusson brought before him, and identify him as the man who carried away Cardillac's corpse.

"Thus: 'I was standing close to the corpse when another man sprang forward, bent down to the body, and hoisted it to his shoulders and carried it away. I have identified Olivier Brusson as this man.' This statement will cause La Régnie to question Brusson afresh. Brusson will not be put to the torture, and further investigation will be made. Then it will be time to approach the king."

Count Miossens carried out D'Andilly's counsel to the letter. Everything went as the lawyer had predicted.

The next move was to approach the king. Brusson's fate was left entirely in Mlle de Scudéry's hands. She put on a black dress of heavy silk, decked herself out in Cardillac's exquisite jewelry, added a long black veil, and thus appeared in Maintenon's apartment at the hour when the king was to be there.

The king's eye caught the glitter of the diamonds in her necklace and armlets. "By heaven, this is Cardillac's jewelry!" Turning to Maintenon, he added: "See, Madame La Marquise, how our lovely bride mourns her bridegroom."

"No," said Mlle de Scudéry, as though pursuing the jest. "I have completely abandoned the goldsmith and would think no more of him, did not the horrifying picture of his murdered body being carried past just in front of me keep appearing to my eyes."

"You saw the poor devil?"

Mlle de Scudéry then told him in a few words how chance had brought her to Cardillac's house after the murder. She described Madelon's grief, and how she had saved the girl from Desgrais's clutches to the cheers of the populace. She described the scenes with La Régnie, Desgrais, and Olivier himself. Before the king had time to gather his wits, Mlle de Scudéry lay at his feet imploring mercy for Olivier Brusson.

"You have astounded me," the king burst out. "That is a frightful story. Who can vouch for the truth of Brusson's account?"

To this Mlle de Scudéry replied: "Miossens's statement. The search of Cardillac's house. An inner conviction. Madelon's virtuous heart that recognized the same virtue in the unhappy Brusson!"

The king walked rapidly up and down a few times, then came and stood in front of Mlle de Scudéry with his hands clasped behind his back.

"I should like to see your Madelon!"

"You have only to give a sign and the little one will be at your feet."

She rushed out and came back with Madelon Cardillac, who was weeping and sobbing with delight and gratitude. Mlle de Scudéry had left Madelon with the Marquise's chambermaid with a short petition drawn up by D'Andilly in her possession. In a few moments she was lying speechless at the king's feet.

Genuinely affected by the child's marvelous beauty, the king raised her and looked at her with eyes bright with tears.

"Isn't the little thing the living image of La Vallière?" Maintenon whispered to Mlle de Scudéry. "The king is revelling in sweet memories. Your game is won."

The king blushed, cast a glance at Maintenon, read the petition, and said gently and kindly:

"I can well believe, dear child, that you are convinced of your loved one's innocence. But let us hear what the Chambre Ardente has to say about it."

He dismissed Madelon, who dissolved in tears. Meanwhile, news of Count Miossen's statement to the Chambre Ardente had got about. The man whom the mob had only a little while earlier cursed as the most villainous of murderers and threatened to tear limb from limb was now lamented as the innocent victim of barbarous justice. Mass processions appeared before La Régnie's palace, shouting threateningly, "Set Olivier Brusson free, he is innocent!" and even throwing stones at the windows.

Several days passed without any fresh information concerning Olivier Brusson's trial. Utterly desolate, Mlle de Scudéry called to see Marquise de Maintenon, who assured her that the king was maintaining complete silence on the matter and that it did not seem advisable to remind him of it.

With D'Andilly's assistance, Mlle de Scudéry found out that the king had secretly had a long talk with Count Miossens. Bontemps, the king's most trusted valet and chargé d'affaires, had been to the Conciergerie and spoken to Brusson. The same Bontemps had been to Cardillac's house one night with several men and had spent a long time there.

Claude Patru, the occupant of the ground floor, stated that there had been a banging and bumping overhead all night long and that he was sure Olivier Brusson had been present, because he had recognized his voice. The king was obviously trying to ascertain the true facts of the case for himself. The long delay in coming to a decision remained incomprehensible. La Régnie must be making every possible effort to prevent his victim from being snatched from between his jaws.

Almost a month had lapsed when the Marquise de Maintenon sent word to Mlle de Scudéry that the king wished to see her in Maintenon's apartment. She told Madelon, who prayed vehemently to the Holy Virgin.

It seemed as though the king had forgotten the whole matter. He passed the time as usual in pleasant conversation with the Marquise de Maintenon and Mlle de Scudéry. At length Bontemps appeared, approached the king, and spoke a few words in a low voice.

The king then rose, walked across to Mlle de Scudéry, and said with radiant eyes:

"I congratulate you, Mademoiselle. Your protégé, Olivier Brusson, is free!"

Mlle de Scudéry burst out into a flood of gratitude. The king interrupted her, informing her that far more ardent thanks awaited her in her own house than he could claim from her, for the happy Olivier was probably at that very minute embracing his Madelon.

"Bontemps," concluded the king, "is to pay over to you a thousand louis. Give them to the little one as a dowry. Let her marry her Brusson, who does not deserve such happiness, but then let them both leave Paris. That is my will."

Martinière hurried to meet Mlle de Scudéry, followed by Baptiste, both of them with faces lit by joy and crying exultantly:

"He is here! He is free! Oh, the dear young people!"

The blissful couple flung themselves at Mlle de Scudéry's feet.

"Oh, I knew that you, and you alone, would save my husband," cried Madelon.

"Oh, faith in you, my mother, was firm in my soul!" cried Olivier.

Both kissed the worthy lady's hands and shed a thousand burning tears. Then they embraced one another again and declared that the supernatural bliss of this moment outweighed all the unspeakable suffering of the immediate past and swore never to part even in death.

A few days later they were bound together by the blessing of a priest. Even if it had not been the king's will, Brusson could not have remained in Paris, where everything reminded him of the atrocious period of Cardillac's crimes, where at any moment some chance might reveal the evil secret—at present known only to a few—and destroy forever his peaceful existence.

Immediately after the wedding, he moved with his young wife to Geneva, taking with him Mlle de Scudéry's blessings. Splendidly equipped through Mademoiselle's dowry, highly gifted in his trade, and possessed of every civil virtue, he quickly built up a happy, carefree life there. The hopes with which his father had gone down disappointed into his grave were fulfilled in him.

A year had passed since Brusson's departure when a public proclamation appeared, signed by Harloy de Chauvalon, Archbishop of Paris, and the advocate of the Court of Parlement, Pierre Arnauld D'Andilly, to the effect that a repentant sinner had surrendered a hoard of stolen jewelry under the secret of the confessional. Anyone who had been robbed of jewelry, especially by a murderous attack in the open street, was invited to report to D'Andilly, and if his description of the jewelry stolen from him tallied exactly with any item found, and there was no doubt about the justice of his claim, the jewelry would be returned to him.

Many of those who figured in Cardillac's list as not having been murdered but merely felled with a blow of the fist called upon the advocate of the Court of Parlement and, to their astonishment, received back the jewelry that had been stolen from them. The rest went to the treasury of the church of Saint-Eustache.

The Killing of Sir John Tyrrell

From *Pelham*

EDWARD BULWER-LYTTON

Known principally for his historical novel *The Last Days of Pompeii (1834)*, Edward Bulwer-Lytton (1803–1873, born Edward Lytton Bulwer, created Lord Lytton in 1866) started out writing trendy novels depicting adventurous rogues—a favorite theme of the day.

In *Pelham* (1828), about three-quarters of the way through a rather flat picaresque romp about a "gentleman" and not a rogue, he turns the formula inside out and creates a murder-mystery sequence involving pursuit and capture of a killer.

In addition, he embellishes his murder-mystery chapters with literary bonuses that have come to be detective novel staples: compelling atmosphere, brooding suspense, and the *feel* of impending doom, which he establishes through descriptions of the countryside that foreshadow both Edgar Allan Poe's "The Fall of the House of Usher" (1839) and A. Conan Doyle's novel *The Hound of the Baskervilles* (1902).

Deduction based on faulty logic is the keynote of the following excerpt from *Pelham*, which acts as a springboard for the conclusion of the novel. The hero misreads circumstantial evidence at the site of the murder and deduces exactly the opposite to what is the truth. Correct deduction and subsequent investigation by the hero then results in a sustained and exciting search in the slums of London for the real murderer.

Chester Park was not many miles distant from Newmarket race-course. On the day of the races, Lord Chester mounted me on one of his horses and I joined the party of house guests.

Our shortest way lay through rather an intricate series of cross-roads. The chief characteristics of the country were broad, dreary plains, diversified at times by dark plantations of fir and larch. The road was rough and stony, and here and there a melancholy rivulet, swelled by the first rains of spring, crossed our path, and lost itself in the rank weeds of some inhospitable marsh.

About six miles from Chester Park, to the left of the road, stood an old house with a new face; the brown, time-honored bricks which composed the fabric were strongly contrasted by large Venetian windows newly inserted in frames of the most ostentatious white. A smart, green veranda, scarcely finished, ran along the low portico, and formed the termination to two thin rows of meagre and dwarfish sycamores.

In spite of these well-mudged and well-thriving graces of art, there was such a comfortless and desolate appearance about the place that it quite froze one to look at it; to be sure, a damp marsh on one side, and the skeleton rafters and beams of an old stable on the other, backed by a few dull and sulky-looking fir-trees, might in some measure create, or at least considerably add to, the indescribable cheerlessness of the *tout ensemble*.

"Will you let me ask whom that cheerful mansion belongs to?" I asked Lord Chester.

"To a Mr. Dawson, whose father was a gentleman farmer who bred horses, a very respectable person."

We proceeded but a few yards before we were stopped by a precipitous ascent. At the foot of the hill was a broad, unenclosed patch of waste land. A heron, flapping its enormous wings as it rose, directed my attention to a pool overgrown with rushes, and half-sheltered on one side by a decayed tree, which, if one might judge from the breadth and hollowness of its trunk, had been a refuge to the wild bird, and a shelter to the wild cattle, at a time when such were the only intruders upon its hospitality.

There was something remarkably singular and grotesque in the shape and sinuosity of its naked and spectral branches; two of exceeding length stretched themselves forth in the very semblance of arms held out in the attitude of supplication; and the bend of the trunk over the desolate pond, the form of the hoary and blasted summit, and the hollow trunk half riven asunder in the shape of limbs, seemed to favor the gigantic deception.

This was the only tree visible; for a turn of the road, and the unevenness of the ground, completely veiled the house we had passed, and a few low firs and sycamores which made its only plantations. The sullen pool, its ghostlike guardian, the dreary heath around, the rude features of the country beyond, and the apparent absence of all habitation—conspired to make a scene of the most dispiriting and striking desolation. I know not how to account for it: but, as I gazed around in silence, the whole place appeared to grow over my mind as one which I had seen, though dimly and drearily, as in a dream, before; and a nameless and unaccountable presentiment of fear and evil sank like ice into my heart.

We ascended the hill; and, the rest of the road being better adapted to expedition, we mended our pace, and soon arrived at the goal of our journey.

The race-ground had its customary complement of knaves and fools—the dupers and the duped. Poor Lady Chester, who had proceeded to the ground by the high-road, was driving to and fro, the very picture of cold and discomfort; and a few solitary carriages which honored the course looked as miserable as if they were witnessing the funeral of their owners' persons rather than the peril of their characters and purses.

Now, then, arose the noise, the clatter, the swearing, the lying, the perjury, the cheating, the crowd, the bustle, the hurry, the rush, the heat, the ardor, the impatience, the hope, the terror, the rapture, the agony of the RACE.

The instant the first heat was over, one asked me one thing, one bellowed another: I fled to Lord Chester; he did not heed me. I took refuge with the marchioness; she was as sullen as the east wind could make her. I was in the lowest pit of despondency, and the devils that kept me there were as blue as Lady Chester's nose. Silent, sad, sorrowful, and sulky, I rode away from the crowd, and moralized on its vicious propensities.

Fortunately, my better angel reminded me that about the distance of three miles from the course lived an old college friend, blessed, since we had met, with a parsonage and a wife. I turned my horse's head and bade adieu to the course.

As I cantered across the far end of the heath, my horse started from an object upon the ground; it was a man wrapped from head to foot in a long horseman's cloak, and so well guarded as to the face, from the raw inclemency of the day, that I could not catch even a glimpse of the features, through the hat and neck-shawl which concealed them. The head was turned, in apparent anxiety, towards the distant throng; and imagining the man belonging to the lower orders, with whom I am always familiar, I addressed to him, *en passant*, some trifling remark on the event of the race. He made no answer. There was something about him which induced me to look back several moments after I had left him behind. He had not moved an inch.

There is such a certain uncomfortableness always occasioned to the mind by stillness and mystery united, that even the disguising garb and motionless silence of the man, innocent as I thought they must have been, impressed themselves disagreeably on my meditation as I rode briskly on.

My visit took up several hours, and when I returned to the heath, I looked anxiously round for the conspicuous equipage of Lady Chester, but in vain. The ground was thin; nearly all the higher orders had retired; the common people, grouped together, and clamoring noisily, were withdrawing; and the shrill voices of the itinerant hawkers of cards and bills had, at length, subsided into silence.

I rode over the ground, in the hope of finding some solitary straggler of our party. Alas! there was no one; and, with much reluctance at, and distaste to, my lonely retreat, I turned in a homeward direction from the course.

The evening had already set in, but there was a moon in the cold, gray sky, that I could almost have thanked, in a sonnet, for a light which I felt was never more welcomely dispensed, when I thought of the cross-roads and dreary country I had to pass before I reached the longed-for haven of Chester Park.

After I had left the direct road, the wind, which had before been piercingly keen, fell, and I perceived a dark cloud behind, which began slowly to overtake my steps. I care little, in general, for the discomfort of a shower; yet, as when we are in one misfortune we always exaggerate the consequence of a new one, I looked upon my dark pursuer with a very impatient and petulant frown, and set my horse on a trot, much more suitable to my inclination than his own.

Indeed, he seemed fully alive to the cornless state of the parson's stable, and evinced his sense of the circumstance by a very languid mode of progression, and a constant attempt, whenever his pace abated, and I suffered the rein to slumber upon his neck, to crop the rank grass that sprang up on either side of our road. I had proceeded about three miles on my way, when I heard the clatter of hoofs behind me. My even pace soon suffered me to be overtaken; and as the stranger checked his horse, when he was nearly by my side, I turned toward him, and beheld Sir John Tyrrell.

[I had first met him when delivering a challenge to a duel from Sir Reginald Glanville, my best friend and brother of my fiancée. Tyrrell had refused to fight. I had no animosity toward him. He was staying at Chester Park as a guest just as I was.]

"Well,"said he, "this is really fortunate; for I began to fear I should have my ride this cold evening entirely to myself."

"I imagined that you had long reached Chester Park by this time," said I. "Did not you leave the course with our party?"

"No," answered Tyrrell; "I had business at Newmarket with a rascally fellow of the name of Dawson. He lost to me rather a considerable wager, and asked me to come to town with him after the race, in order to pay me. As he said he lived on the direct road to Chester Park, and would direct and even accompany me through all the difficult parts of the ride, I the less regretted not joining Chester and his party; and you know, Pelham, that when pleasure pulls one way and money another, it is all over with the first.

"Well—to return to my rascal—would you believe that when we got to Newmarket he left me at the inn, in order, he said, to fetch the money; and after having kept me in a cold room with a smoky chimney for more than an hour without making his appearance, I sallied out into the town, and found Mr. Dawson quietly seated in a hall with that scoundrel Thornton, whom I did not conceive, till then, he was acquainted with. It seems that he was to win, at hazard, sufficient to pay his wager!

"You may fancy my anger and the consequent increase to it, when he rose from the table, approached me, expressed his sorrow, d—d his ill-luck, and informed me that he could not pay me for three months. You know that I could not ride home with such a fellow; he might have robbed me by the way: so I returned to my inn, dined, ordered my horse, set off, inquired my way of every passenger I passed, and after innumerable misdirections—here I am!"

"I cannot sympathize with you," said I, "since I am benefited by your misfortunes. But do you think it very necessary to trot so fast? I fear my horse can scarcely keep up with yours."

Tyrrell cast an impatient glance at my panting steed. "It is cursed unlucky you should be so badly mounted, and we shall have a pelting shower presently."

In complaisance to Tyrrell, I endeavored to accelerate my steed. The roads were rough and stony; and I had scarcely got the tired animal into a sharp trot, before—whether or no by some wrench among the deep ruts and flinty causeway—he fell suddenly lame. The impetuosity of Tyrrell broke out in oaths, and we both dismounted to examine the cause of my horse's hurt, in the hope that it might only be the intrusion of some pebble between the shoe and the hoof.

While we were yet investigating the cause of our misfortune, two men on horseback overtook us. Tyrrell looked up. "By Heaven," said he in a low tone, "it's that dog Dawson and his worthy coadjutor Tom Thornton."

"What's the matter, gentlemen?" cried the bluff voice of the latter. "Can I be of any assistance?" and without waiting our reply, he dismounted and came up to us. He had no sooner felt the horse's leg than he assured us it was a most severe strain and that the utmost I could effect would be to walk the brute gently home.

As Tyrrell broke out into impatient violence at this speech, the sharper looked up at him with an expression of countenance I by no means liked, but in a very civil and even respectful tone, said, "If you wish, Sir John, to reach Chester Park sooner than Mr. Pelham can possibly do, suppose you ride on with us; I will put you in the direct road before I quit you." (Good breeding, thought I, to propose leaving me to find my own way through this labyrinth of ruts and stones!) However, Tyrrell, who was in a vile humor, refused the offer, in no very courteous manner; and added that he should continue with me as long as he could, and did not doubt that when he left me he should be able to find his own way. Thornton pressed the invitation still closer, and even offered, *sotto voce*, to send Dawson on before, should the baronet object to his company.

"Pray, sir," said Tyrrell, "leave me alone and busy yourself about your own affairs." After so tart a reply, Thornton thought it useless to say more; he remounted, and with a silent and swaggering nod of familiarity, soon rode away with his companion.

"I am sorry," said I, as we were slowly proceeding, "that you rejected Thornton's offer."

"Why, to say the truth," answered Tyrrell, "I have so very bad an opinion of him that I was almost afraid to trust myself in his company on so dreary a road. I have nearly (and he knows it) to the amount of two thousand pounds about me; for I was very fortunate in my betting-book today."

"I know nothing about racing regulations," said I; "but I thought one never paid sums of that amount upon the ground?"

"Ah!" answered Tyrrell, "but I won this sum, which is eighteen hundred pounds, of a country squire from Norfolk, who said he did not know when he should see me again, and insisted on paying me on the spot: 'faith, I was not nice in the matter. Thornton was standing by at the time, and I did not half like the turn of his eye when he saw me put it up. Do you know, too," continued Tyrrell after a pause, "that I had a d—d fellow dodging me all day, and yesterday too; wherever I go I am sure to see him. He seems constantly, though distantly, to follow me; and what is worse, he wraps himself up so well, and keeps at so cautious a distance, that I can never catch a glimpse of his face."

I know not why, but at that moment the recollection of the muffled figure I had seen upon the course flashed upon me.

"Does he wear a long horseman's cloak?"

"He does," answered Tyrrell, in surprise; "have you observed him?"

"I saw such a person on the race-ground," replied I, "but only for an instant!"

Further conversation was suspended by a few heavy drops which fell upon us; the cloud had passed over the moon, and was hastening rapidly and loweringly over our heads. Tyrrell was neither of an age, a frame, nor a temper, to be so indifferent to a hearty wetting as myself.

"Come, come," he cried, "you *must* put on that beast of yours. I can't get wet for all the horses in the world."

I was not much pleased with the dictatorial tone of this remark. "It is impossible," said I, "especially as the horse is not my own, and seems considerably lamer than at first; but let me not detain you."

"Well!" cried Tyrrell in a raised and angry voice, which pleased me still less than his former remark; "but how am I to find my way if I leave you?"

"Keep straight on," said I, "for a mile farther, then a sign-post will direct you to the left; after a short time you will have a steep hill to descend, at the bottom of which is a large pool and a singularly-shaped tree; then again keep straight on, till you pass a house belonging to Mr. Dawson—"

"Hang it, Pelham, make haste!" exclaimed Tyrrell impatiently, as the rain began now to descend fast and heavy.

"When you have passed that house," I resumed coolly, rather enjoying his petulance, "you must bear to the right for six miles, and you will be at Chester Park in less than an hour."

Tyrrell made no reply, but put spurs to his horse. The pattering rain and the angry heavens soon drowned the last echoes of the receding hoof-clang.

For myself, I looked in vain for a tree, not even a shrub was to be found; the fields lay bare on either side, with no other partition but a dead hedge and a deep dike. "Melius fit patientia," etc., thought I, as Horace said. "What cannot be removed, becomes lighter by patience." Presently, for I think scarcely five minutes had elapsed since Tyrrell's departure, a horseman passed me at a sharp pace: the moon was hid by the dense cloud; and the night, though not wholly dark, was dim and obscured, so that I could only catch the outline of the flitting figure. A thrill of fear crept over me when I saw that it was enveloped in a horseman's cloak.

I soon rallied. "There are more cloaks in the world than one," said I to myself; "besides, even if it be Tyrrell's dodger, as he calls him, the baronet is better mounted than any highwayman since the days of Du Val; and is, moreover, strong enough and cunning enough to take admirable care of himself."

With such meditations I endeavored to beguile the time, and cheat myself into forgetfulness of the lameness of my horse and the dripping wetness of his rider. At last the storm began sullenly to subside; one impetuous torrent, tenfold more violent than those that had preceded it, was followed by a momentary stillness, which was again broken by a short relapse of a less formidable severity, and, the moment it ceased, the beautiful moon broke out, the cloud rolled heavily away, and the sky shone forth, as fair and smiling as Lady —— at a ball, after she has been beating her husband at home.

But at that instant, or perhaps a second before the storm ceased, I thought I heard the sound of a human cry. I paused, and my heart stood still; I could have heard a gnat hum: the sound was not repeated; my ear caught nothing but the plashing of the rain-drops from the dead hedges, and the murmur of the swollen dikes, as the waters pent within them rolled hurriedly on.

By and by, an owl came suddenly from behind me, and screamed as it flapped across my path; that, too, went rapidly away: and with a smile at what I deemed my own fancy, I renewed my journey.

I soon came to the precipitous descent I have before mentioned; I dismounted, for safety, from my drooping and jaded horse, and led him down the hill. At a distance beyond I saw something dark moving on the grass which bordered the road: as I advanced, it started forth from the shadow, and fled rapidly before me, in the moonshine; it was a riderless horse.

A chilling foreboding seized me: I looked round for some weapon, such as the hedge might afford; and finding a strong stick of tolerable weight and thickness, I proceeded more cautiously, but more fearlessly than before. As I wound down the hill, the moonlight fell full upon the remarkable and lonely tree I had observed in the morning. Bare, wan, and giantlike, as it rose amidst the surrounding waste, it borrowed even a more startling and ghostly appearance from the cold and lifeless moonbeams which fell around and upon it like a shroud. The retreating steed I had driven before me paused by this tree.

I hastened my steps, as if by an involuntary impulse, as well as the enfeebled animal I was leading would allow me, and discovered a horseman galloping across the waste at full speed. The ground over which he passed was steeped in the moonshine, and I saw the long and disguising cloak, in which he was enveloped, as clearly as by the light of day.

I paused; and as I was following him with my looks, my eye fell upon some obscure object by the left side of the pool. I threw my horse's rein over the hedge, and firmly grasping my stick, hastened to the spot. As I approached the object I perceived that it was a human figure: it was lying still and motionless; the limbs were half immersed in the water; the face was turned upwards; the side and throat were wet with a deep red stain—it was of blood: the thin, dark hairs of the head were clotted together over a frightful and disfiguring contusion.

I bent over the face in a shuddering and freezing silence. It was the countenance of Sir John Tyrrell!

I took up the heavy hand: it fell from my grasp; and as it did so, I thought a change passed over the livid countenance. I was deceived; it was but a light cloud flitting over the moon; it rolled away, and the placid and guiltless light shone over that scene of dread and blood, making more wild and chilling the eternal contrast of earth and heaven—man and his Maker, passion and immutability, death and eternal life.

The house I had noted in the morning was, as I knew, within a few minutes' walk of the spot; but it belonged to Dawson, upon whom the first weight of my suspicions rested. I called to mind the disreputable character of that man, and the still more daring and hardened one of his companion Thornton.

I remembered the reluctance of the deceased to accompany them and the well-grounded reason he assigned; and my suspicions amounting to certainty, I resolved rather to proceed to Chester Park, and there give the alarm, than to run the unnecessary risk of interrupting the murderers in the very lair of their retreat. And yet, thought I, as I turned slowly away, how, if they were the villains, is the appearance and flight of the disguised horseman to be accounted for?

Then flashed upon my recollection all that Tyrrell had said of the dogged pursuit of that mysterious person, and the circumstance of his having passed me upon the road so immediately after Tyrrell had quitted me. These reflections (associated with a name that I did not dare breathe even to myself, although I could not suppress a suspicion which accounted at once for the pursuit, and even for the deed) made me waver in, and almost renounce, my former condemnation of Thornton and his friend; and by the time I reached the white gate and dwarfish avenue which led to Dawson's house, I resolved, at all events, to halt at the solitary mansion, and mark the effect my information would cause.

A momentary fear for my own safety came across me, but was as instantly dismissed; for even supposing the friends were guilty, still it would be no object to them to extend their remorseless villainy to me; and I knew that I could sufficiently command my own thoughts to prevent any suspicion I might form from mounting to my countenance or discovering itself in my manner.

There was a light in the upper story; it burned still and motionless. How holy seemed the tranquility of life contrasted with the forced and fearful silence of the death scene I had just witnessed! I rang twice at the door; no one came to answer my summons, but the light in the upper window moved hurriedly to and fro.

"They are coming," said I to myself. No such thing; the casement above was opened; I looked up, and discovered to my infinite comfort and delight, a blunderbuss protruded eight inches out of the window in a direct line with my head; I receded close to the wall with no common precipitation.

"Get away, you rascal," said a gruff but trembling voice, "or I'll blow your brains out."

"My good sir," I replied, still keeping my situation, "I come on urgent business, either to Mr. Thornton or Mr. Dawson; and you had better, therefore, if the delay is not very inconvenient, defer the honor you offer me till I have delivered my message."

"Master and 'Squire Thornton are not returned from Newmarket, and we cannot let any one in till they come home," replied the voice, in a tone somewhat mollified by my rational remonstrance; and while I was deliberating what rejoinder to make, a rough, red head, like Liston's in a farce, poked itself cautiously out under cover of the blunderbuss, and seemed to reconnoiter my horse and myself. Presently another head, but attired in the more civilized gear of a cap and flowers, peeped over the first person's left shoulder; the view appeared to reassure them both.

"Sir," said the female, "my husband and Mr. Thornton are not returned; and we have been so much alarmed of late by an attack on the house that I cannot admit any one till their return."

"Madam," I replied, reverently doffing my hat, "I do not like to alarm you by mentioning the information I should have given to Mr. Dawson; only oblige me by telling them, on their return, to look beside the pool on the common: they will then do as best pleases them."

Upon this speech, which certainly was of no agreeable tendency, the blunderbuss palpitated so violently, that I thought it highly imprudent to tarry any longer in so perilous a vicinity; accordingly, I made the best of my way out of the avenue, and once more resumed my road to Chester Park.

I arrived there at length; the gentlemen were still in the dining-room. I sent out for Lord Chester, and communicated the scene I had witnessed, and the cause of my delay.

"What! Brown Bob lamed?" said he, "and Tyrrell—poor—poor fellow, how shocking! We must send instantly. Here, John! Tom! Wilson!" and his lordship shouted and rang the bell in an indescribable agitation.

The under butler appeared, and Lord Chester began: "My head groom—Sir John Tyrrell is murdered—violent sprain in off leg—send lights with Mr. Pelham—poor gentleman—an express instantly to Dr. Physicon—Mr. Pelham will tell you all—Brown Bob—his throat cut from ear to ear—what shall be done?" and with this coherent and explanatory harangue, the marquis sank down in his chair in a sort of hysteric.

The under butler looked at him in suspicious bewilderment.

"Come," said I, "I will explain what his lordship means"; and, taking the man out of the room, I gave him in brief the necessary particulars. I ordered a fresh horse for myself, and four horsemen to accompany me. While these were preparing the news was rapidly spreading, and I was soon surrounded by the whole house. Many of the gentlemen wished to accompany me; and Lord Chester, who had at last recovered from his stupor, insisted upon heading the search. We set off, to the number of fourteen, and soon arrived at Dawson's house; the light in the upper room was still burning. We rang, and after a brief pause Thornton himself opened the door to us. He looked pale and agitated.

"How shocking!" he said directly; "we are only just returned from the spot."

"Accompany us, Mr. Thornton," said I sternly, and fixing my eye upon him.

"Certainly," was his immediate answer, without testifying any confusion; "I will fetch my hat." He went into the house for a moment.

"Do you suspect these people?" whispered Lord Chester.

"Not suspect," said I, "but *doubt*."

We proceeded down the avenue: "Where is Mr. Dawson?" said I to Thornton.

"Oh, within!" answered Thornton. "Shall I fetch him?"

"Do," was my brief reply.

Thornton was absent some minutes; when he reappeared, Dawson was following him. "Poor fellow," said he to me in a low tone; "he was so shocked by the sight that he is still all in a panic; besides, as you will see, he is half-drunk still."

I made no answer, but looked narrowly at Dawson; he was evidently, as Thornton said, greatly intoxicated; his eyes swam, and his feet staggered as he approached us; yet, through all the natural effects of drunkenness, he seemed nervous and frightened. This, however, might be the natural (and consequently innocent) effect of the mere sight of an object so full of horror; and, accordingly, I laid little stress upon it.

We reached the fatal spot; the body seemed perfectly unmoved. "Why," said I, apart to Thornton, while all the rest were crowding fearfully round the corpse, "why did you not take the body within?"

"I was going to return here with our servant for that purpose," answered the gambler; "for poor Dawson was both too drunk and too nervous to give me any assistance."

"And how came it," I rejoined, eyeing him searchingly, "that you and your friend had not returned home when I called there, although you had both long since passed me on the road, and I had never overtaken you?"

Thornton, without any hesitation, replied: "Because, during the violence of the shower, we cut across the fields to an old shed, which we recollected, and we remained there till the rain had ceased."

"They are probably innocent," thought I; and I turned to look once more at the body, which our companions had now raised. There was upon the head a strong contusion, as if inflicted by some blunt and heavy instrument. The fingers of the right hand were deeply gashed, and one of them almost dissevered: the unfortunate man had, in all probability, grasped the sharp weapon from which his other wounds proceeded: these were one wide cut along the throat, and another in the side; either of them would have occasioned his death.

In loosening the clothes, another wound was discovered, but apparently of a less fatal nature; and in lifting the body, the broken blade of a long sharp instrument, like a case-knife [a sheath knife] was discovered. It was the opinion of the surgeon who afterwards examined the body that the blade had been broken by coming in contact with one of the rib bones; and it was by this that he accounted for the slightness of the last-mentioned wound.

I looked carefully among the fern and long grass to see if I could discover any other token of the murderer: Thornton assisted me. At the distance of some feet from the body I thought I perceived something glitter. I hastened to the place, and picked up a miniature. I was just going to cry out, when Thornton whispered: "Hush! I know the picture; it is as I suspected!"

An icy thrill ran through my heart. With a desperate but trembling hand, I cleansed from the picture the blood in which, notwithstanding its distance from the corpse, the greater part of it was bathed. I looked upon the features; they were those of a young and singularly beautiful female. I recognized them not: I turned to the other side of the miniature; upon it were braided two locks of hair—one was the long, dark ringlet of a woman, the other was of a lighter auburn. Beneath were four letters. I looked eagerly at them. "My eyes are dim," said I, in a low tone to Thornton, "I cannot trace the initials."

"But *I* can," replied he, in the same whispered key, but with a savage exultation, which made my heart stand still: "they are G.D., R.G.; they are the initials of Gertrude Douglas and *Reginald Glanville.*"

I looked up at the speaker; our eyes met; I grasped his hand vehemently. He understood me. "Put it up," said he; "we will keep the secret." All this, so long in the recital, passed in the rapidity of a moment.

"Have you found anything there, Pelham?" shouted one of our companions.

"No!" cried I, thrusting the miniature into my bosom, and turning unconcernedly away.

We carried the corpse to Dawson's house. The poor wife was in fits. We heard her scream as we laid the body upon a table in the parlor.

"What more can be done?" said Lord Chester.

"Nothing," was the general answer. No excitement makes people insensible to the chance of catching cold.

"Let us go home, then, and send to the nearest magistrate," exclaimed our host; and this proposal required no repetition.

On our way, Chester said to me, "That fellow Dawson looked devilish uneasy; don't you still suspect him and his friend?"

"I *do not!*" answered I, emphatically.

Ignoring the fallibility of circumstantial evidence, Pelham deduces (correctly) that his friend Glanville, whom he has suspected of being the cloaked horseman, has been at the scene of the crime and, because he knows Glanville hates Tyrrell, deduces (incorrectly) that he has killed him. Convinced of Glanville's innocence after his capture and confrontation, Pelham spends the remainder of the novel—much more gripping and exciting than the beginning—in searching out the real murderer.

The Clue
of the Paper Scrap

From *The Memoirs of Vidocq*

EUGÈNE FRANÇOIS VIDOCQ

Translated by Edwin Gile Rich

Adapted by the editor

Eugène François Vidocq (1775–1857) started out life as a professional criminal—he was a convict at the age of twenty-one—and later turned secret agent for the head of the Criminal Department of the Paris Police. Eventually he reorganized the department and created the Sûreté, Paris's model police system. In 1811 he became *Chef de la Sûreté*. Vidocq had a genuine flair for publicity, and in 1828 the first volume of his *Mémoires* appeared, penned by an anonymous writer, although purportedly corrected and approved by Vidocq himself. Though somewhat romanticized, the anecdotes were all based on true cases that Vidocq had solved.

At the age of fifty, Vidocq left the Sûreté and founded one of the first private detective agencies. It was not a success. His life foundered after he left the Sûreté. But he was not forgotten. He reappeared often in fiction—as Vautrin (Balzac's *Le Pére Goriot*, 1834), as Javert (in Hugo's *Les Miserables*, 1862), as Favart (in Bulwer-Lytton's *Night and Morning*, 1845), as Lecocq (in Gaboriau; see page 181), and perhaps in many other incarnations as well.

For about four months a large number of murders and robberies had been committed on the roads near the capital without any indication as to the identity of the criminals. It was in vain that the police kept watch over certain suspects. Their surveillance was unsuccessful, until one particular crime led to the eventual capture of the guilty parties.

A butcher named Fontaine, who lived at Courtille, was going home from a fair at Corbeil, carrying a money bag in which he had fifteen hundred francs. He had passed Cour-de-France and was walking in the direction of Essonne, when, a short distance from an inn where he had stopped, he met two men rather neatly dressed. The sun was setting, and Fontaine was not averse to traveling in company. He greeted the two unknowns, and at once got into conversation with them.

"Good evening, messieurs," he said.

"Good evening, friend," they answered.

The colloquy continued. "It's almost dark and I still have a good bit of road to travel."

"Where are you going, if we're not too curious?"

"To Milly to buy sheep."

"In that case, if you'll permit us, we'll go along with you. Since we're going to Corbeil, it couldn't be better."

"That's true," the butcher answered. "It couldn't be better. I'll take advantage of your company. When one has money on one, you see, it's better not to be alone."

"Oh. You have money?"

"A rather large sum."

"We have some too, but we don't think there's any danger in this area."

"I have something to defend myself with," the butcher said, showing a stick, "and with you two along, robbers would look twice, wouldn't they?"

"They'd not meddle with us."

"No, by God, they'd not!"

Talking away in this manner, the three arrived at the door of a small house decorated with a branch of juniper that identified it as a pub. Fontaine proposed to his companions that they buy a bottle. They went in and purchased Beaugency, eight sous a liter, and sat down at a table. In honor of the occasion they had more than one bottle.

When there was no further reason to prolong their stay, each one wanted to pay the bill. Three-quarters of an hour went by, and when they did finally leave, Fontaine, who had imbibed a bit too much, was cheerful and feeling no pain. In such a situation, what man could nurse distrust of others?

Fontaine congratulated himself on having found such bon vivants for companions. Believing that there was nothing better to do than to accept them for guides, he put himself in their hands and the three were soon on a secondary road.

The butcher walked in front with one of the unknowns; the other followed closely. Darkness was now complete. One could scarcely see four yards. But crime has the eyes of a lynx; it pierces the thickest darkness.

Fontaine was expecting nothing. The bon vivant and good companion to his rear struck him a heavy blow with his club. Fontaine reeled. He tried to turn around and strike back, but a second blow leveled him. At the same moment the other brigand, armed with a dagger, hurled himself on him and stabbed him repeatedly. Fontaine fought back as well as he could, but in the end he sank down.

The bandits then took his money bag, rifled it, and ran, leaving him bathed in blood. A passing traveler heard his groans. The fresh air had revived him. The traveler approached, promptly gave him first aid, and hurried to ask for help at the nearest house.

The magistrates at Corbeil were alerted immediately. The king's prosecutor arrived on the scene of the attack, questioned the people present, and inquired into all the circumstances.

Twenty-eight wounds, more or less serious, attested to what extent the thieves had feared that their victim would escape. However, Fontaine could speak faintly, but was too weak to give all the information needed by the law. The investigators took him to the hospital, and two days afterwards a notable improvement in his situation gave hope that he might survive.

The removal of the victim had been made with the most minute exactness; nothing had been neglected which might lead to the discovery of the assassins. Footprints had been traced on paper.

Buttons and bits of paper covered with blood had been collected. On one of these fragments of paper found not far away there were some characters traced by hand, but they seemed to have no connection with the crime and could furnish no clear lead for the investigation.

However, the king's prosecutor did attach a high importance to these scraps of paper. His men again explored the vicinity where Fontaine had been lying, and a second bit of paper, which appeared to be part of an address torn from some document, was picked up in the grass. By examining it carefully, they managed to make out these words, or parts of words:

Monsieur Rao
   Merchand de Vins,
      Bar   Roche
               Cli

This scrap of paper seemed to have formed part of a document of some kind, but its exact nature was impossible to determine. On such an occasion even the slightest detail might provide important evidence.

The magistrates who assembled these first bits and pieces of evidence deserved praise for the zeal and skill they displayed. As soon as they had fulfilled the first part of their responsibility, they went in all haste to Paris to inform the judicial and administrative authorities.

On their request I was brought into the case, and, furnished with the report they had drawn up, I began to prepare my own search to find the would-be murderers.

The victim had described them on his bed at the hospital, but I doubted that I could rely wholly on such information. Few men in great danger preserve enough presence of mind to observe details accurately, and I was disposed to suspect the testimony of Fontaine because it was almost too precise.

He related that during the struggle, which had lasted some time, one of his assailants had fallen to his knees and cried out in immediate pain. A moment later, he told his accomplice that he was suffering cruel pains. Other remarks which Fontaine thought he had heard appeared to me extraordinary, given the state he was in. It was difficult for me to believe that he was accurate in his recollections. Nevertheless, I proposed to profit by them. First, however, it was necessary to adopt a more positive point of departure for my investigation.

The ragged part of the address on the paper scrap was, in my opinion, a puzzle that must be solved before further effort. I put my mind at work, and without too much effort, since I knew a great deal about the environs of Paris, reconstructed a possible address:

> *Monsieur Raoul,*
>> *Merchand de Vins,*
>>> *Barrière Rochechouart,*
>>>> *Chaussée de Clignancourt*

Or:

> *Mister Raoul,*
>> *Wine Merchant,*
>>> *Rochechouart Turnpike,*
>>>> *Clignancourt Road*

It was evident that the thieves had been in touch with a wine merchant in that particular place. Perhaps the wine merchant himself was one of the robbers.

I did, in fact, know "Raoul." His full name was Clair Raoul. He kept a wine shop which was reputed to be a hangout for some of the most intrepid smugglers in the business. His pub was notorious in the area. Not only that, but Raoul's wife was the sister of a freed convict. I knew he was acquainted with all sorts of evildoers with records. In a word, his reputation was odoriferous. When a crime was committed, one could say, without fear of contradiction, "If it wasn't you, it was your brother or one of your relatives."

Raoul was always under suspicion for one thing or another, either on his own account, or on that of his associates. Resolved to keep the approaches to his pub watched, I ordered my agents to keep an eye on everyone who frequented it to discover anyone with a bad knee wound.

While my observers were at their posts, I learned that Raoul habitually received at his place one or two good-for-nothing fellows of bad appearance with whom he seemed to be intimately connected. The neighbors affirmed that they always went out together, that their absences were frequent, and that most of Raoul's commerce was contraband. A wine merchant who lived nearby told me that he had noticed Raoul often going out at dusk and not returning until the morning, sometimes worn out with fatigue and covered with mud.

I was also told that Raoul had a target set up in his garden, and that he practiced firing his pistol there. Such was the gossip that came to me from all sides.

At the same time my agents reported that they had seen a man whom they presumed to be one of the bandits at Raoul's. He did not limp, but walked painfully, and his dress was similar to Fontaine's description. The agents added that this man was constantly accompanied by his wife, and that the two were in close contact with Raoul. They were said to live on the first floor of a house on Rue Coquenard.

However, to prevent alerting them to our suspicions, my agents had not pushed the investigation any further. This report strengthened my own convictions. I had no sooner received it than I placed my agents on watch at the house they had designated.

I waited until daylight, and even before it appeared, I was on picket duty at the Rue Coquenard site. I stayed there until four o'clock in the afternoon. I was beginning to grow impatient when my agents pointed out to me a man whose name and features were familiar to me. His name was Court.

"That's the man," they said. Scarcely had I seen Court than I recalled his dossier and was convinced that he was one of the bandits who had attacked and robbed Fontaine.

Court had just finished several months in jail, and I recalled that I had arrested him for fraud with violence some time in the past. He was one of those unfortunate beings who, like Cain, bore the sentence of death on their foreheads.

Without being much of a prophet, one could have predicted that he was destined for the gallows. I had a presentiment that he was about to reach the end of his perilous career. However, I did not want to act too precipitately. I wanted to find out whether he had any legitimate means of support.

No one knew of any, and the neighbors whom I questioned all agreed that his conduct was a bit irregular. Like Raoul, Court could be regarded as a hardened criminal. One would have condemned them both on appearances alone. I had reason to see them both as downright scoundrels and I hastened to get warrants that would authorize their seizure.

The following day, before sunrise, I was in Court's home. When I reached the landing, I knocked on his door.

"Who's there?" he asked.

"Open!" I said, imitating Raoul's voice. "It's Raoul."

I heard him hurrying, and when he opened the door, supposing he was talking to Raoul, Court asked, "Is there anything new?"

"Yes," I answered. "There's something new."

He saw me and froze. "Oh!" he exclaimed. "It's Monsieur Jules." That was the name the girls and thieves gave me.

Court's wife appeared, as astonished as he was. "Monsieur Jules!"

"Are you afraid?" I asked. "I'm not as black as the devil."

"That's true," Court admitted. "Monsieur Jules is all right. He's arrested me once, but that's all right—I'm not annoyed."

"I believe you," I answered. "Is it my fault that you smuggle?"

"Smuggle?" Court repeated in the assured accents of a man from whom a great weight has been lifted. "Smuggle! Oh, Monsieur Jules, you know that if I did, I should not hide it from you. Besides, you can search."

While he became more and more at ease, I searched the lodging, where I found a pair of loaded pistols, knives, garments which appeared to have been freshly washed, and some other objects which I took.

Now I had to complete the investigation. If I arrested the husband and left the wife free, there was no doubt that she would warn Raoul. So I took them both to the nearest police station, Place Cadet. I held Court in custody and he suddenly became somber and thoughtful. The precautions I had taken caused him uneasiness; his wife also seemed worried. They were both stricken when, once at the station, I recommended that they be separated and watched.

When Court was questioned, he responded merely by a shake of the head. He was eighteen hours without touching a mouthful of food. He kept his eyes fixed in space, his features immobile. I recognized the symptoms. This impassivity indicated to me that the man was guilty. In such circumstances I had already remarked two extremes of behavior: a dreary silence, or an unendurable volubility.

Court and his wife were now in custody. It remained only for me to take Raoul.

I went to his place but found that he was not there. The waiter who looked after the shop told me that Raoul had slept in Paris where he had lodgings, but that, since it was Sunday, he would come in early.

Raoul's absence was a setback I had not foreseen. I trembled at the thought that he might take a notion to see his friend Court. In that case he would certainly be told of his arrest, and it was probable that he would vanish. I was afraid also that he might have seen us on the Rue Coquenard, and my apprehensions doubled when the waiter told me that his lodgings were in the Faubourg Montmartre.

The waiter had never been there, and could not tell me about the place, but he presumed that it was around Place Cadet. Each bit of information he gave me confirmed my fears. Perhaps Raoul was late because he had suspected something.

By nine o'clock he had not returned. I questioned the waiter again, but without saying anything which would inspire suspicion. The waiter could not understand why Raoul was not working behind his counter. He was obviously uneasy at Raoul's absence. The maid who prepared breakfast for my agents and myself expressed astonishment that her master, and especially her mistress, were not on the spot. She was afraid that they had met with some accident.

"If I knew their address," she said, "I'd go and see whether they were all right."

I was sure that they were, but what had become of them? At noon we were still without news, and I definitely believed that our secret was out. The waiter, who had been on watch at the door for a moment, ran in. "There he is!"

"Who wants me?" asked Raoul.

He had scarcely crossed the threshold when he recognized me.

"Ah, bonjour, Monsieur Jules! What brings you to our quarter today?"

He was far from thinking that I had business with him. In order to allay his fears, I tried to put him completely off the scent.

"Oh, a small matter," I said. "About your decision to become a liberal."

"A liberal?" Raoul was puzzled.

"What's more, they say you.... We can't talk here. Can we speak privately?"

"Certainly. Up on the first floor. I'll follow."

I went up the stairs, signalling to my agents to watch Raoul, and to seize him if he made any move to escape. The wretch did not even consider it; he came immediately as he had promised. His air was almost jovial. I was delighted to see him so unsuspecting.

"Now we're alone," I said, "we can talk at our ease. Can't you guess why I've come?"

"Really, I can't."

"You've already caused trouble with those song parties you hold, which you insist on holding in your pub, in spite of the fact that they're against the law. The police say that every Sunday you hold meetings here and sing songs against the government. Not only do you allow in crowds of suspects, but you have large numbers in from noon to four o'clock.

"The police also say you have in your hands a mass of seditious and immoral songs that are only handed out to people well known to you. I am disturbed to be charged with such a disagreeable mission. I did not know that it was you who owned the pub, or I should have excused myself. As far as that goes, it's better that I should be here than someone else. I don't wish you harm. The best thing for you to do is to give me all the songs you have. Then, to avoid trouble, I would advise you not to receive men here whose political opinions might compromise you."

"I did not know," Raoul observed slyly, "that politics was your department."

"When one is in the service of the government, one has to do a little bit of everything."

He smiled. "In other words, you do what you're told. That's all one to me. As true as my name's Clair Raoul, I can swear to you that I have been denounced falsely. I'm only trying to make a living. Stay here all day. You'll see we don't sing any bad songs."

"I consent—but no spree, at least. Have someone get rid of the songs, and no word of this will get out. If you want the singers—"

"What do you take me for?" Raoul replied. "If I give my word, I'll never go back on it. One either has honor or one hasn't. Besides, to prove that my intentions aren't bad, you needn't leave me. I promise not to whisper a word, not even to my wife when she comes back—of that you can be sure. Now you must let me cut up the meats."

"With pleasure. I don't want to stop your business. I could even lend you a hand."

"You're too good, Monsieur Jules!"

"Come on. To work!"

We went downstairs together. Raoul armed himself with a large cleaver. I rolled up my sleeves to the elbows, tied an apron on, and helped cut up the veal destined to delight the Luculluses of Raoul's pub. From the veal I turned to lamb, and sliced dozens of cutlets. When there was nothing more to be done in the kitchen, I went into the cellar and helped make wine at six sous a liter.

All during this operation I was face to face with Raoul and I stuck to him like glue. I confess that several times I trembled lest he suspect the reason why I kept such close watch on him. If he had suspected, he would certainly have cut my throat. But in me he saw only a familiar face which belonged to the law, and he was perfectly at ease in regard to any accusations that might be directed at him.

I had performed the duties of a second chef for four hours when the commissioner of police, whom I had alerted, arrived at last. As soon as I saw him, I hurried over and chatted with him in a low voice. Then I went back to Raoul.

"It's the commissioner," I said. "They want us at your place in Paris. Not here."

"Then let's go there."

"Whatever we do, we'll have to come back here. Why don't you ask the commissioner to search the pub now? If he finds nothing, he'll think you've been wrongly suspected."

Raoul followed my advice and suggested the commissioner make his search immediately. It produced nothing.

"Well," said Raoul, with an air of satisfaction, "will you help me clean up the mess you've made? If I'd committed murder, it could be little worse than what you've done!"

The assurance with which he uttered the last phrase disconcerted me. I almost felt some doubts about his guilt. Yet I knew he was a murderer, and the favorable impression was promptly erased from my mind. It was sad to think that this scoundrel, with his hands still reeking of his victim's blood, could say such a thing so cooly in front of his accusers. Raoul was calm and almost triumphant. When we got into the cab to go to his apartment in Paris, one would have thought he was going to a wedding.

"My wife will be surprised to see me in such good company," he laughed.

She came to the door to let us in. On seeing us, her face remained imperturbable. She offered us seats politely. We had no time to lose, so without regard to etiquet, the commissioner and I proceeded to search the apartment. Raoul was present. He guided us about with a kind of cool affability.

In order to make my cock-and-bull story about the illegal song sheets somewhat believable, we attached the greatest importance to Raoul's papers. He gave me the key to his writing desk. I took up a bundle of sheets, and the first one I saw was a court summons which had been delivered to him fairly recently. The top left hand part of the sheet had been torn off. In my mind's eye I could retrace the form of the scrap on which was written the name and address that I had filled in from the paper found at the scene of Fontaine's assault. I knew the two pieces would fit together exactly.

I showed the summons to the commissioner. Raoul had been watching us with indifference as we examined the summons. But suddenly his muscles contracted. He grew pale, and, jumping toward a drawer of his commode, he tried to seize one of his loaded pistols kept there. My agents hurled themselves on him and disarmed him quickly.

We had all the evidence we needed.

It was midnight when Clair Raoul and his wife were taken to police headquarters. Court was brought in a quarter of an hour later from Place Cadet. The two accomplices were locked up separately. Until now we had only presumptions, some evidence, and half-proofs against them.

I proposed to get each of them to confess separately while they were still unaware of what we had on them. I tried my eloquence first on Court. I used every sort of argument to convince him that it was in his own best interest to confess.

"Tell the truth," I said. "Why do you persist in denying what we know? At the first interrogation you undergo, you will find that we know more than you think. Not all the people you attacked are dead. Some of them will testify against you. Even if you keep silent, you'll be condemned nonetheless. The scaffold isn't what's the most terrible; it's the torment, the inflexibility of your confinement. If you haven't confessed, the magistrates will leave you neither peace nor quiet until the hour of your execution. If you remain silent, prison will be hell for you. If, on the contrary, you speak, show repentance and resignation, then the judges may pity you and treat you with a great deal of lenience."

Court was much disturbed. When I told him that all the people he attacked were not dead, he changed color and turned his head away. Imperceptibly he had lost countenance. His breathing increased visibly, then he found difficulty in catching a breath.

Finally, at half-past four in the morning, he gave up, fell on my neck, the tears flowing abundantly.

"Oh, Monsieur Jules," he exclaimed between sobs. "I am a great sinner. I'll tell you all."

I was careful not to specify to Court what crime he was accused of committing. As probably he had murdered more than once, I did not want to isolate any one victim. I hoped that by using vague terms, and in avoiding precise information, we would get information of some crimes other than that of Fontaine.

Court reflected a moment. "Well, yes," he said finally. "I murdered the poultry dealer. He must have had nine lives. The poor devil, to recover from such an assault! This is how it was done, Monsieur Jules—may I die if I lie. There were several travelers who were returning after selling their merchandise in Paris. I thought they were loaded with money. Consequently I lay in wait for them. I stopped the first two who presented themselves, but I found almost nothing on them.

"When I was on the verge of giving it up in despair, I heard the noise of a carriage. I ran to it. It was the poultry dealer. I surprised him half asleep. I ordered him to give me his purse. He searched and I searched myself. He had only eighty francs. Eighty francs! I ask you, what was that to me? I had the rent to pay. The owner had threatened to put me out. And to add to my misfortune, I was harassed by other creditors. I was overcome with rage. I took my pistols and fired them both into the breast of that gentleman. A fortnight later I got the news that he was still alive. Judge my surprise. Since that moment I haven't had an instant's rest. I suspected that he would play me some bad turn."

"Your fears are well founded," I said. "But the poultry dealer was not the only one you assaulted. There is that butcher whom you stabbed after you'd taken his money bag."

"As for that," Court said, "may God have his soul! I'll answer that if he deposes against me, it will be the Last Judgement."

"You're mistaken. The butcher didn't die."

"Oh, so much the better!" Court cried.

"No, he will not die. I must warn you that he has described you and your accomplice so that there can be no mistake."

Court maintained again that he had no accomplice, but he hadn't the strength to persist in the lie for long. He ended by naming Clair Raoul. I knew that there might be others, and insisted he name them, but it was in vain. I had to be content with the confession he had made. For fear that he would retract his statement later, I immediately called the commissioner and in his presence had Court reiterate what he had told me in every detail.

Doubtless it was a great victory to have induced Court to confess his guilt and sign his declaration, but we were not through yet. Raoul must be persuaded to follow the example of his friend.

In the end I succeeded in doing exactly that. I brought the two of them together. They embraced. Court said to Raoul, "So you've done as I did, and confessed? You've done well."

For an instant Raoul was as if annihilated, but soon recovered his spirits.

"By Jove, Monsieur Jules," he said, "that's well played. You've done me in handsomely. As I am a man of my word, I'll do what I told you and hide nothing."

Immediately he began to dictate a statement which confirmed that of his accomplice. When the commissioner had received the new revelations in the form demanded by the law, I stayed to talk with the two murderers.

They supped well and drank reasonably. Their faces had become calm. There was no trace of animosity in them. They saw that the matter was concluded. When they confessed, they had agreed to pay their debt to society.

The Purloined Letter

EDGAR ALLAN POE

Nil sapientiae odiosius acumine nimio. —Seneca

In three short stories, "The Murders in the Rue Morgue" (1841), "The Mystery of Marie Roget" (1842), and "The Purloined Letter" (1845), Edgar Allan Poe (1809–1849) laid down the rules for the detective story. He took what Herodotus, Voltaire, Vidocq, Hoffmann, Bulwer-Lytton, and others had all toyed with as part of a story, and formulated it into a *primary* story element. *And* created the detective short story, the tale devoted exclusively to the solution of a criminal problem. In "The Purloined Letter" Poe lets Dupin (his incarnation of Vidocq) elaborate on the detective's knowledge of human nature and his psychological understanding of the way the mind works. In no other work does any writer explain so succinctly the manner of "getting under the criminal's skin" to anticipate his moves. The solution of the mystery—indeed a slight one—is held to the end of the story. The main thrust of the narrative lies in Dupin's discussion of the reading of character and intellect, and his exposition of the psychology of deduction and detection. No one has ever done it better. Yet, unaccountably, Poe dropped the formula he had invented and moved into the realm of the horror story in his few remaining years.

Incidentally, the quotation at the head of the story translates as "Nothing is more detestable to good sense than too much subtlety." Attributed to Seneca, mysteriously, the quotation is *not* in the Latin dramatist's works at all. Only Poe knows where it really came from.

At Paris, just after dark one gusty evening in the autumn of 18—, I was enjoying the twofold luxury of meditation and a meerschaum, in company with my friend C. Auguste Dupin, in his little back library, or book-closet, *au troisième, No. 33 Rue Dunôt, Faubourg St. Germain*. For one hour at least we had maintained a profound silence; while each, to any casual observer, might have seemed intently and exclusively occupied with the curling eddies of smoke that oppressed the atmosphere of the chamber. For myself, however, I was mentally discussing certain topics which had formed matter for conversation between us at an earlier period of the evening; I mean the affair of the Rue Morgue, and the mystery attending the murder of Marie Roget. I looked upon it, therefore, as something of a coincidence, when the door of our apartment was thrown open and admitted our old acquaintance, Monsieur G——, the Prefect of the Parisian police.

We gave him a hearty welcome; for there was nearly half as much of the entertaining as of the contemptible about the man, and we had not seen him for several years. We had been sitting in the dark, and Dupin now arose for the purpose of lighting a lamp, but sat down again, without doing so, upon G.'s saying that he had called to consult us, or rather to ask the opinion of my friend, about some official business which had occasioned a great deal of trouble.

"If it is any point requiring reflection," observed Dupin, as he forbore to enkindle the wick, "we shall examine it to better purpose in the dark."

"That is another of your odd notions," said the prefect, who had a fashion of calling every thing "odd" that was beyond his comprehension, and thus lived amid an absolute legion of "oddities."

"Very true," said Dupin, as he supplied his visitor with a pipe, and rolled towards him a comfortable chair.

"And what is the difficulty now?" I asked. "Nothing more in the assassination way, I hope?"

"Oh no; nothing of that nature. The fact is, the business is very simple indeed, and I make no doubt that we can manage it sufficiently well ourselves; but then I thought Dupin would like to hear the details of it, because it is so excessively *odd*."

"Simple and odd," said Dupin.

"Why, yes; and not exactly that either. The fact is, we have all been a good deal puzzled because the affair *is* so simple, and yet baffles us altogether."

"Perhaps it is the very simplicity of the thing which puts you at fault," said my friend.

"What nonsense you *do* talk!" replied the prefect, laughing heartily.

"Perhaps the mystery is a little *too* plain," said Dupin.

"Oh, good heavens! who ever heard of such an idea?"

"A little *too* self-evident."

"Ha! ha! ha!—ha! ha! ha!—ho! ho! ho!" roared our visitor, profoundly amused, "oh, Dupin, you will be the death of me yet!"

"And what, after all, *is* the matter on hand?" I asked.

"Why, I will tell you," replied the prefect, as he gave a long, steady, and contemplative puff, and settled himself in his chair. "I will tell you in a few words; but, before I begin, let me caution you that this is an affair demanding the greatest secrecy, and that I should most probably lose the position I now hold, were it known that I confided it to any one."

"Proceed," said I.

"Or not," said Dupin.

"Well, then; I have received personal information, from a very high quarter, that a certain document of the last importance, has been purloined from the royal apartments. The individual who purloined it is known; this beyond a doubt; he was seen to take it. It is known, also, that it still remains in his possession."

"How is this known?" asked Dupin.

"It is clearly inferred," replied the prefect, "from the nature of the document, and from the non-appearance of certain results which would at once arise from its passing *out* of the robber's possession; that is to say, from his employing it as he must design in the end to employ it."

"Be a little more explicit," I said.

"Well, I may venture so far as to say that the paper gives its holder a certain power in a certain quarter where such power is immensely valuable." The prefect was fond of the cant of diplomacy.

"Still I do not quite understand," said Dupin.

"No? Well; the disclosure of the document to a third person, who shall be nameless, would bring in question the honor of a personage of most exalted station; and this fact gives the holder of the document an ascendancy over the illustrious personage whose honor and peace are so jeopardized."

"But this ascendancy," I interposed, "would depend upon the robber's knowledge of the loser's knowledge of the robber. Who would dare—"

"The thief," said G., "is the Minister D——, who dares all things, those unbecoming as well as those becoming a man. The method of the theft was not less ingenious than bold. The document in question—a letter, to be frank—had been received by the personage robbed while alone in the royal *boudoir*. During its perusal she was suddenly interrupted by the entrance of the other exalted personage from whom especially it was her wish to conceal it. After a hurried and vain endeavor to thrust it in a drawer, she was forced to place it, open it was, upon a table. The address, however, was uppermost, and, the contents thus unexposed, the letter escaped notice. At this juncture enters the Minister D——. His lynx eye immediately perceives the paper, recognizes the handwriting of the address, observes the confusion of the personage addressed, and fathoms her secret. After some business transactions, hurried through in his ordinary manner, he produces a letter somewhat similar to the one in question, opens it, pretends to read it, and then places it in close juxtaposition to the other. Again he converses, for some fifteen minutes, upon the public affairs. At length, in taking leave, he takes also from the table the letter to which he had no claim. Its rightful owner saw, but, of course, dared not call attention to the act, in the presence of the third personage who stood at her elbow. The minister decamped; leaving his own letter—one of no importance—upon the table."

"Here, then," said Dupin to me, "you have precisely what you demand to make the ascendary complete—the robber's knowledge of the loser's knowledge of the robber."

"Yes," replied the prefect; "and the power thus attained had, for some months past, been wielded, for political purposes, to a very dangerous extent. The personage robbed is more thoroughly convinced, every day, of the necessity of reclaiming her letter. But this, of course, cannot be done openly. In fine, driven to despair, she has committed the matter to me."

"Than whom," said Dupin, amid a perfect whirlwind of smoke, "no more sagacious agent could, I suppose, be desired, or even imagined."

"You flatter me," replied the prefect; "but it is possible that some such opinion may have been entertained."

"It is clear," said I, "as you observe, that the letter is still in the possession of the minister; since it is this possession, and not any employment of the letter, which bestows the power. With the employment the power departs."

"True," said G.; "and upon this conviction I proceeded. My first care was to make thorough search of the minister's hotel; and here my chief embarrassment lay in the necessity of searching without his knowledge. Beyond all things, I have been warned of the danger which would result from giving him reason to suspect our design."

"But," said I, "you are quite *au fait* in these investigations. The Parisian police have done this thing often before."

"O yes; and for this reason I did not despair. The habits of the minister gave me, too, a great advantage. He is frequently absent from home all night. His servants are by no means numerous. They sleep at a distance from their master's apartment, and being chiefly Neapolitans, are readily made drunk. I have keys, as you know, with which I can open any chamber or cabinet in Paris. For three months a night has not passed, during the greater part of which I have not been engaged, personally, in ransacking the D—— Hotel. My honor is interested, and, to mention a great secret, the reward is enormous. So I did not abandon the search until I had become fully satisfied that the thief is a more astute man than myself. I fancy that I have investigated every nook and corner of the premises in which it is possible that the paper can be concealed."

"But is it not possible," I suggested, "that although the letter may be in possession of the minister, as it unquestionably is, he may have concealed it elsewhere than upon his own premises?"

"This is barely possible," said Dupin. "The present peculiar condition of affairs at court, and especially of those intrigues in which D—— is known to be involved, would render the instant availability of the document—its susceptibility of being produced at a moment's notice—a point of nearly equal importance with its possession."

"Its susceptibility of being produced?" said I.

"That is to say, of being *destroyed*," said Dupin.

"True," I observed; "the paper is clearly then upon the

premises. As for its being upon the person of the minister, we may consider that as out of the question."

"Entirely," said the prefect. "He had been twice waylaid, as if by foot-pads, and his person rigorously searched under my own inspection."

"You might have spared yourself this trouble," said Dupin. "D——, I presume is not altogether a fool, and, if not, must have anticipated these waylayings, as a matter of course."

"Not *altogether* a fool," said G., "but then he is a poet, which I take to be only one remove from a fool."

"True," said Dupin, after a long and thoughtful whiff from his meerschaum, "although I have been guilty of certain doggerel myself."

"Suppose you detail," said I, "the particulars of your search."

"Why the fact is, we took our time, and we searched *everywhere*. I have had long experience in these affairs. I took the entire building, room by room; devoting the nights of a whole week to each. We examined, first, the furniture of each apartment. We opened every possible drawer; and I presume you know that, to a properly trained police agent, such a thing as a *secret* drawer is impossible. Any man is a dolt who permits a 'secret' drawer to escape him in a search of this kind. The thing is *so* plain. There is a certain amount of bulk—of space—to be accounted for in every cabinet. Then we have accurate rules. The fiftieth part of a line could not escape us. After the cabinets we took the chairs. The cushions we probed with the fine long needles you have seen me employ. From the tables we removed the tops."

"Why so?"

"Sometimes the top of a table, or other similarly arranged piece of furniture, is removed by the person wishing to conceal an article; then the leg is excavated, the article deposited within the cavity, and the top replaced. The bottoms and tops of bedposts are employed in the same way."

"But could not the cavity be detected by sounding?" I asked.

"By no means, if, when the article is deposited, a sufficient wadding of cotton be placed around it. Besides, in our case, we were obliged to proceed without noise."

"But you could not have removed—you could not have taken to pieces *all* articles of furniture in which it would have been possible to make a deposit in the manner you mention. A letter may be compressed into a thin spiral roll, not differing much in shape or bulk from a large knitting-needle, and in this form it might be inserted into the rung of a chair, for example. You did not take to pieces all the chairs?"

"Certainly not; but we did better—we examined the rungs of every chair in the hotel, and indeed the jointings of every description of furniture, by the aid of a most powerful microscope. Had there been any traces of recent disturbance we should not have failed to detect it instantly. A single grain of gimlet-dust, for example, would have been as obvious as an apple. Any disorder in the glueing—any unusual gaping in the joints—would have sufficed to insure detection."

"I presume you looked to the mirrors, between the boards and the plates, and you probed the beds and the bed-clothes, as well as the curtains and carpets."

"That of course; and when we had absolutely completed every particle of the furniture in this way, then we examined the house itself. We divided its entire surface into compartments, which we numbered, so that none might be missed; then we scrutinized each individual square inch throughout the premises, including the two houses immediately adjoining, with the microscope as before."

"The two houses adjoining!" I exclaimed; "you must have had a great deal of trouble."

"We had; but the reward offered is prodigious."

"You included the *grounds* around the houses?"

"All the grounds are paved with brick. They gave us comparatively little trouble. We examined the moss between the bricks, and found it undisturbed."

"You looked among D——'s papers, of course, and into the books of the library?"

"Certainly; we opened every package and parcel; we not only opened every book, but we turned over every leaf in each volume, not contenting ourselves with a mere shake, according to the fashion of some of our police officers. We also measured the thickness of every book-*cover*, with the most accurate admeasurement, and applied to each the most jealous scrutiny of the microscope. Had any of the bindings been recently meddled with, it would have been utterly impossible that the fact should have escaped observation.

Some five or six volumes, just from the hands of the binder, we carefully probed, longitudinally, with the needles."

"You explored the floors beneath the carpets?"

"Beyond doubt. We removed every carpet, and examined the boards with the microscope."

"And the paper on the walls?"

"Yes."

"You looked into the cellars?"

"We did."

"Then," I said, "you have been making a miscalculation, and the letter is *not* upon the premises as you suppose."

"I fear you are right there," said the prefect. "And now, Dupin, what would you advise me to do?"

"To make a thorough re-search of the premises."

"That is absolutely needless," replied G——, "I am not more sure that I breathe than I am that the letter is not at the hotel."

"I have no better advice to give you," said Dupin. "You have, of course, an accurate description of that letter?"

"Oh, yes!"—And here the prefect, producing a memorandum-book, proceeded to read aloud a minute account of the internal, and especially of the external, appearance of the missing document. Soon after finishing the perusal of this description, he took his departure, more entirely depressed in spirits than I had ever known the good gentleman before.

In about a month afterward he paid us another visit, and found us occupied very nearly as before. He took a pipe and a chair and entered into some ordinary conversation. At length I said:

"Well, but G——, what of the purloined letter? I presume you have at last made up your mind that this is no such thing as overreaching the minister?"

"Confound him, say I—yes; I made the re-examination, how-ever, as Dupin suggested—but it was all labor lost, as I knew it would be."

"How much was the reward offered, did you say?" asked Dupin.

"Why, a very great deal—a *very* liberal reward—I don't like to say how much, precisely; but one thing I *will* say, that I wouldn't mind giving my individual check for fifty thousand francs to any one who could obtain me that letter. The fact is, it is becoming of more and more importance every day; and the reward has been lately doubled. If it were trebled, however, I could no more than I have done."

"Why, yes," said Dupin, drawlingly, between the whiffs of his meerschaum, "I really—think, G——, you have not exerted yourself—to the utmost in this matter. You might—do a little more, I think, eh?"

"How?—in what way?"

"Why—puff, puff—you might—puff, puff—employ counsel in the matter, eh?—puff, puff, puff. Do you remember the story they tell of Abernethy?"

"No, hang Abernethy!"

"To be sure! hang him and welcome. But, once upon a time, a certain rich miser conceived the design of sponging upon this Abernethy for a medical opinion. Getting up, for this purpose, an ordinary conversation in a private company, he insinuated his case to the physician, as that of an imaginary individual.

"'We will suppose,' said the miser, 'that his symptoms are such and such; now, doctor, what would *you* have directed him to take?'

"'Take!' said Abernethy, 'why, take *advice*, to be sure.'"

"But," said the prefect, a little discomposed, "I am *perfectly* willing to take advice, and to pay for it. I would *really* give fifty thousand francs to any one who would aid me in the matter."

"In that case," replied Dupin, opening a drawer, and producing a check-book, "you may as well fill me up a check for the amount you mentioned. When you have signed it, I will hand you the letter."

I was astounded. The prefect appeared absolutely thunder-stricken. For some minutes he remained speechless and motionless, looking incredulously at my friend with open mouth, and eyes that seemed starting from their sockets; then, apparently recovering himself in some measure, he seized a pen, and after several pauses and vacant stares, finally filled up and signed a check for fifty thousand francs, and handed it across the table to Dupin. The latter examined it carefully and deposited it in his pocket-book; then, unlocking an *escritoire*, took thence a letter and gave it to the prefect. This functionary grasped it in a perfect agony of joy, opened it with a trembling hand, cast a rapid glance at its contents, and then, scrambling and struggling to the door, rushed at length unceremoniously from the room and from the house, without having uttered a syllable since Dupin had requested him to fill up the check.

When he had gone, my friend entered into some explanation.

"The Parisian police," he said, "are exceedingly able in their way. They are persevering, ingenious, cunning, and thoroughly versed in the knowledge which their duties seem chiefly to demand. Thus, when G—— detailed to us his mode of searching the premises at the Hotel D——, I felt entire confidence in his having made a satisfactory investigation—so far as his labors extended."

"So far as his labors extended?" said I.

"Yes," said Dupin. "The measures adopted were not only the best of their kind, but carried out to absolute perfection. Had the letter been deposited within the range of their search, these fellows would, beyond a question, have found it."

I merely laughed—but he seemed quite serious in all that he said.

"The measures, then," he continued, "were good in their kind, and well executed; their defect lay in their being inapplicable to the case, and to the man. A certain set of highly ingenious resources are, with the prefect, a sort of Procrustean bed, to which he forcibly adapts his designs. But he perpetually errs by being too deep or too shallow, for the matter in hand; and many a schoolboy is a better reasoner than he. I knew one about eight years of age, whose success at guessing in the game of 'even and odd' attracted universal admiration. This game is simple, and is played with marbles. One player holds in his hand a number of these toys, and demands of another whether the number is even or odd. If the guess is right, the guesser wins one; if wrong, he loses one. The boy to whom I allude won all the marbles of the school. Of course he had some principle of guessing; and this lay in mere observation and admeasurement of the astuteness of his opponents. For example, an arrant simpleton is his opponent, and, holding up his closed hand, asks: 'Are they even or odd?' Our schoolboy replies, 'Odd,' and loses; but upon the second trial he wins, for he then says to himself, 'The simpleton had them even upon the first trial, and his amount of cunning is just sufficient to make him have them odd upon the second; I will therefore guess odd'; he guesses odd, and wins. Now, with a simpleton a degree above the first, he would have reasoned thus: 'This fellow finds that in the first instance I guessed odd, and, in the second, he will propose to himself upon the first impulse, a simple variation from even to odd, as did the first simpleton; but then a second thought will suggest that this is too simple a variation, and finally he will decide upon putting it even as before. I will therefore guess even'; he guesses even, and wins. Now this mode of reasoning in the schoolboy, whom his fellows termed 'lucky'—what, in its last analysis, is it?"

"It is merely," I said, "an identification of the reasoner's intellect with that of his opponent."

"It is," said Dupin; "and, upon inquiring of the boy by what means he effected the *thorough* identification in which his success consisted, I received answer as follows: 'When I wish to find out how wise, or how stupid, or how good, or how wicked is any one, of what are his thoughts at the moment, I fashion the expression on my face, as accurately as possible, in accordance with the expression of his, and then wait to see what thoughts or sentiments arise in my mind or heart, as if to match or correspond with the expression.' This response of the schoolboy lies at the bottom of all the spurious profundity which has been attributed to Rochefoucault, to La Bougive, to Machiavelli, and to Campanella."

"And the identification," I said, "of the reasoner's intellect with that of his opponent, depends, if I understand you aright, upon the accuracy with which the opponent's intellect is admeasured."

"For its practical value it depends upon this," replied Dupin; "and the prefect and his cohort fail so frequently, first, by default of this identification, and secondly, by ill-admeasurement, or rather through non-admeasurement, of the intellect with which they are engaged. They consider only their *own* ideas of ingenuity; and, in searching for anything hidden, advert only to the modes in which *they* would have hidden it. They are right in this much—that their own ingenuity is a faithful representative of that of *the mass*; but when the cunning of the individual felon is diverse in character from their own, the felon foils them, of course. This always happens when it is above their own, and very usually when it is below. They have no variation of principle in their investigations; at best, when urged by some unusual emergency—by some extraordinary reward—they extend or exaggerate their old modes of *practice*, without touching their principles. What, for example, in this case of D——, has been done to vary the principle of action? What is all this boring, and probing, and sounding, and scrutinizing with the microscope, and

dividing the surface of the building into registered square inches—
what is it all but an exaggeration *of the application* of one principle or
set of principles of search, which are based upon the one set of notions
regarding human ingenuity, to which the prefect, in the long routine
of his duty, has been accustomed? Do you not see he has taken it for
granted that *all* men proceed to conceal a letter—not exactly in a
gimlet-hole bored in a chair-leg—but, at least in *some* out-of-the-way
hole or corner suggested by the same tenor of thought which would
urge a man to secrete a letter in a gimlet-hole bored in a chair-leg?
And do you not see also, that such *recherchés* nooks for concealment
are adapted only for ordinary occasions, and would be adopted only
by ordinary intellects; for, in all cases of concealment, a disposal of
the article concealed—a disposal of it in this *recherche* manner—is, in
the very first instance, presumable and presumed; and thus its
discovery depends, not at all upon the acumen, but altogether upon
the mere care, patience, and determination of the seekers, and where
the case is of importance—or, what amounts to the same thing in the
policial eyes, when the reward is of magnitude, the qualities in
question have *never* been known to fail. You will now understand
what I meant in suggesting that, had the purloined letter been hidden
anywhere within the limits of the prefect's examination—in other
words, had the principle of its concealment been comprehended
within the principles of the prefect—its discovery would have been a
matter altogether beyond question. This functionary, however, has
been thoroughly mystified; and the remote source of his defeat lies in
the supposition that the minister is a fool, because he has acquired
renown as a poet. All fools are poets; this the prefect *feels*; and he is
merely guilty of a *non distributio medii* in thence inferring that all poets
are fools."

"But is this really the poet?" I asked. "There are two brothers, I
know; and both have attained reputation in letters. The minister I
believe has written learnedly on the differential calculus. He is a
mathematician, and no poet."

"You are mistaken; I know him well; he is both. As poet *and*
mathematician, he would reason well; as mere mathematician, he
could not have reasoned at all, and thus would have been at the mercy
of the prefect."

"You surprise me," I said, "by these opinions, which have been
contradicted by the voice of the world. You do not mean to set at

naught the well-digested idea of centuries. The mathematical reason
has long been regarded as *the* reason *par excellence.*"

"'*Il y a à parier,*'" replied Dupin, quoting from Chamfort, "'*que
toute idée publique, toute convention reçue, est une sottise, car elle a
convenue au plus grand nombre.*' The mathematicians, I grant you,
have done their best to promulgate the popular error to which you
allude, and which is none the less an error for its promulgation as a
truth. With an art worthy a better cause, for example, they have
insinuated the term 'analysis' into the application to algebra. The
French are the originators of this particular deception; but if a term is
of any importance—if words derive any value from applicability—
then 'analysis' conveys 'algebra' about as much as, in Latin, '*ambitus*'
implies 'ambition,' '*religio*' 'religion,' or '*homines honesti,*' a set of
honorable men."

"You have a quarrel on hand, I see," said I, "with some of the
algebraists of Paris; but proceed."

"I dispute the availability, and thus the value, of that reason
which is cultivated in any especial form other than the abstractly
logical. I dispute, in particular, the reason educed by mathematical
study. The mathematics are the science of form and quantity;
mathematical reasoning is merely logic applied to observation upon
form and quantity. The great error lies in supposing that even the
truths of what is called *pure* algebra, are abstract or general truths.
And this error is so egregious that I am confounded at the
universality with which it has been received. Mathematical axioms
are *not* axioms of general truth. What is true of *relation*—of form and
quantity—is often grossly false in regard to morals, for example. In
this latter science it is very usually *un*true that the aggregated parts are
equal to the whole. In chemistry also the axiom fails. In the
consideration of motive it fails; for two motives, each of a given
value, have not, necessarily, a value when united, equal to the sum of
their values apart. There are numerous other mathematical truths
which are only truths within the limits of *relation.* But the mathematician argues from his *finite truths,* through habit, as if they were of an
absolutely general applicability—as the world indeed imagines them
to be. Bryant, in his very learned 'Mythology,' mentions an
analogous source of error, when he says that 'although the Pagan
fables are not believed, yet we forget ourselves continually, and make
inferences from them as existing realities.' With the algebraists,

however, who are Pagans themselves, the 'Pagan fables' *are* believed, and the inferences are made, not so much through lapse of memory as through an unaccountable addling of the brains. In short, I never yet encountered the mere mathematician who would be trusted out of equal roots, or one who did not clandestinely hold it as a point of his faith that $x^2 + px$ was absolutely and unconditionally equal to q. Say to one of these gentlemen, by way of experiment, if you please, that you believe occasions may occur where $x^2 + px$ is *not* altogether equal to q, and, having made him understand what you mean, get out of his reach as speedily as convenient, for, beyond doubt, he will endeavor to knock you down.

"I mean to say," continued Dupin, while I merely laughed at his last observations, "that if the minister had been no more than a mathematician, the prefect would have been under no necessity of giving me this check. I knew him, however, as both mathematician and poet, and my measures were adapted to his capacity, with reference to the circumstances by which he was surrounded. I knew him as a courtier, too, and as a bold *intriguant*. Such a man, I considered, could not fail to be aware of the ordinary policial modes of action. He could not have failed to anticipate—and events have proved that he did not fail to anticipate—the waylayings to which he was subjected. He must have foreseen, I reflected, the secret investigations of his premises. His frequent absences from home at night, which were hailed by the prefect as certain aids to his success, I regarded only as *ruses*, to afford opportunity for thorough search to the police, and thus the sooner to impress them with the conviction to which G——, in fact, did finally arrive—the conviction that the letter was not upon the premises. I felt, also, that the whole train of thought, which I was at some pains in detailing to you just now, concerning the invariable principle of policial action in searches for articles concealed—I felt that this whole train of thought would necessarily pass through the mind of the minister. It would impera- tively lead him to despise all the ordinary *nooks* of concealment. *He* could not, I reflected, be so weak as not to see that the most intricate and remote recess of his hotel would be as open as his commonest closets to the eyes, to the probes, to the gimlets, and to the microscopes of the prefect. I saw, in fine, that he would be driven, as a matter of course, to simplicity, if not deliberately induced as a matter of choice. You will remember, perhaps, how desperately the prefect laughed when I suggested, upon our first interview, that it was just possible this mystery troubled him so much on account of its being so *very* self-evident."

"Yes," said I, "I remember his merriment well. I really thought he would have fallen into convulsions."

"The material world," continued Dupin, "abounds with very strict analogies to the immaterial; and thus some color or truth has been given to the rhetorical dogma, that metaphor, or simile, may be made to strengthen an argument as well as to embellish a description. The principle of the *vis inertiae*, for example, seems to be identical in physics and metaphysics. It is not more true in the former, that a large body is with more difficulty set in motion than a smaller one, and that its subsequent *momentum* is commensurate with this difficulty, than it is, in the latter, that intellects of the vaster capacity, while more forcible, more constant, and more eventful in their movements than those of inferior grade, are yet less readily moved, and more embarrassed and full of hesitation in the first few steps of their progress. Again: have you ever noticed which of the street signs, over the shop doors, are the most attractive to attention?"

"I have never given the matter a thought," I said.

"There is a game of puzzles," he resumed, "which is played upon a map. One party playing requires another to find a given word—the name of town, river, state or empire—any word, in short, upon the motley and perplexed surface of the chart. A novice in the game generally seeks to embarrass his opponents by giving them the most minutely lettered names; but the adept selects such words as stretch, in large characters, from one end of the chart to the other. These, like the over-largely lettered signs and placards of the street, escape observation by dint of being excessively obvious; and here the physical oversight is precisely analogous with the moral inapprehension by which the intellect suffers to pass unnoticed those considerations which are too obtrusively and too palpably self-evident. But this is a point, it appears, somewhat above or beneath the understanding of the prefect. He never once thought it probable, or possible, that the minister had deposited the letter immediately beneath the nose of the whole world, by way of best preventing any portion of that world from perceiving it.

"But the more I reflected upon the daring, dashing, and discriminating ingenuity of D——; upon the fact that the document must always have been *at hand*, if he intended to use it to good purpose; and upon the decisive evidence, obtained by the prefect, that it was not hidden within the limits of that dignitary's ordinary search—the more satisfied I became that to conceal this letter, the minister had resorted to the comprehensive and sagacious expedient of not attempting to conceal it at all.

"Full of these ideas, I prepared myself with a pair of green spectacles, and called one fine morning, quite by accident, at the ministerial hotel. I found D—— at home, yawning, lounging, and dawdling, as usual, and pretending to be in the last extremity of *ennui*. He is, perhaps, the most really energetic human being now alive—but that is only when nobody sees him.

"To be even with him, I complained of my weak eyes, and lamented the necessity of the spectacles, under cover of which I cautiously and thoroughly surveyed the whole apartment, while seemingly intent only upon the conversation of my host.

"I paid especial attention to a large writing-table near which he sat, and upon which lay confusedly, some miscellaneous letters and other papers, with one or two musical instruments and a few books. Here, however, after a long and very deliberate scrutiny, I saw nothing to excite particular suspicion.

"At length my eyes, in going the circuit of the room, fell upon a trumpery filigree card-rack of pasteboard, that hung dangling by a dirty blue ribbon, from a little brass knob just beneath the middle of the mantel-piece. In this rack, which had three or four compartments, were five or six visiting cards and a solitary letter. This last was much soiled and crumpled. It was torn nearly in two, across the middle—as if a design, in the first instance, to tear it entirely up as worthless, had been altered, or stayed, in the second. It had a large black seal, bearing the D—— cipher *very* conspicuously, and was addressed, in a diminutive female hand, to D——, the minister, himself. It was thrust carelessly, and even, as it seemed, contemptuously, into one of the upper divisions of the rack.

"No sooner had I glanced at this letter than I concluded it to be that of which I was in search. To be sure, it was, to all appearance, radically different from the one of which the prefect had read us so minute a description. Here the seal was large and black, with the D—— cipher; there it was small and red, with the ducal arms of the S—— family. Here, the address, to the minister was diminutive and feminine; there the superscription, to a certain royal personage, was markedly bold and decided; the size alone formed a point of correspondence. But, then, the *radicalness* of these differences, which was excessive; the dirt; the soiled and torn condition of the paper, so inconsistent with the *true* methodical habits of D——, and so suggestive of a design to delude the beholder into an idea of the worthlessness of the document; these things, together with the hyperobtrusive situation of this document, full in the view of every visitor, and thus exactly in accordance with the conclusions to which I had previously arrived; these things, I say, were strongly corroborative of suspicion, in one who came with the intention to suspect.

"I protracted my visit as long as possible, and while I maintained a most animated discussion with the minister, upon a topic which I knew well had never failed to interest and excite him, I kept my attention really riveted upon the letter. In this examination, I committed to memory its external appearance and arrangement in the rack; and also fell, at length, upon a discovery which set at rest whatever trivial doubt I might have entertained. In scrutinizing the edges of the paper, I observed them to be more *chafed* than seemed necessary. They presented the *broken* appearance which is manifested with stiff paper, having been once folded and pressed with a folder, is refolded in a reversed direction, in the same creases or edges which had formed the original fold. This discovery was sufficient. It was clear to me that the letter had been turned, as a glove, inside out, re-directed, and re-sealed. I bade the minister good morning, and took my departure at once, leaving a gold snuff-box upon the table.

"The next morning I called for the snuff-box, when we resumed quite eagerly, the conversation of the preceding day. While thus engaged, however, a loud report, as if of a pistol, was heard immediately beneath the windows of the hotel, and was succeeded by a series of fearful screams, and the shoutings of a mob. D—— rushed to the casement, threw it open, and looked out. In the meantime I stepped to the card-rack, took the letter, put it in my pocket, and replaced it by a *fac-simile* (so far as regards externals) which I had carefully prepared at my lodging; imitating the D—— cipher, very readily, by means of a seal formed of bread.

"The disturbance in the street had been occasioned by the frantic behavior of a man with a musket. He had fired it among a crowd of women and children. It proved, however, to have been without ball, and the fellow was suffered to go his way as a lunatic or a drunkard. When he had gone, D—— came from the window, whither I had followed him immediately upon securing the object in view. Soon afterward I bade him farewell. The pretended lunatic was a man in my own pay."

"But what purpose had you," I asked, "in replacing the letter by *fac-simile?* Would it not have been better, at the first visit, to have seized it openly, and departed?"

"D——," replied Dupin, "is a desperate man, and a man of nerve. His hotel, too, is not without attendants devoted to his interests. Had I made the wild attempt you suggest, I might never have left the ministerial presence alive. The good people of Paris might have heard of me no more. But I had an object apart from these considerations. You know my political prepossessions. In this matter, I act as a partisan of the lady concerned. For eighteen months the minister has had her in his power. She has now him in hers; since, being unaware that the letter is not in his possession, he will proceed with his exactions as if it was. Thus will he inevitably commit himself, at once, to his political destruction. His downfall, too, will not be more precipitate than awkward. It is all very well to talk about the *facilis descensus Averni*; but in all kinds of climbing, as Catalani said of singing, it is far more easy to get up than to come down. In the present instance I have no sympathy—at least no pity—for him who descends. He is that *monstrum horrendum*, an unprincipled man of genius. I confess, however, that I should like very well to know the precise character of his thoughts, when, being defied by her whom the prefect terms 'a certain personage,' he is reduced to opening the letter which I left for him in the card-rack."

"How? did you put any thing particular in it?"

"Why—it did not seem altogether right to leave the interior blank—that would have been insulting. D——, at Vienna once, did me an evil turn, which I told him quite good-humoredly, that I should remember. So, as I knew he would feel some curiosity in regard to the identity of the person who had outwitted him, I thought it a pity not to give him a clue. He is well acquainted with my MS., and I just copied into the middle of the blank sheet the words—

> —*Un dessein si funeste,*
> *S'il nest digne d'Atrée, est digne de Thyeste.*

> [*A plan so mournful,*
> *If it is not worthy of Atreus, is worthy of Thyestes.*]

They are to be found in Crébillon's 'Atrée,'"

Duel in the Bois-Rochin

From *The Man in the Iron Mask*

ALEXANDRE DUMAS

Translated from the original French

Alexandre Dumas (1802–1870), master of the swashbuck-
ling historical romance and author of the prototype revenge
novel *The Count of Monte Cristo* (1844–5), loved to write
scenes of palace intrigue. Intrigue to him was only one step
away from police detection, so popular in France and
permeating the works of E.T.A. Hoffmann, Vidocq, and
Poe. In *The Man in the Iron Mask* (1848–50), he toyed with
an old rumor of royal substitution, made possible by the
supposed birth of twin princelings—a cliché of many
mystery novels to come. Episodes of investigation appear in
the long novel, usually featuring D'Artagnan, the king's
musketeer.

In effect, D'Artagnan becomes a secret agent for the
king to spy out mysterious fortifications at Belle-Isle being
erected by one of his close musketeer friends. But
D'Artagnan is also employed in another fashion in this
excerpt. Here he performs a masterful deduction, based on
interpretation of spoor, and reveals the truth about a duel in
the woods. But the king uses his deductions to ferret out and
determine a great many more hidden truths of palace
intrigue. In the end D'Artagnan's true deduction becomes
an untruth, and a blatant lie becomes the official truth.

"Monsieur D'Artagnan," said the king, "you will leave this place by the little door of the private staircase."

"Yes, sire."

"You will mount your horse."

"Yes sire."

"And you will proceed to the Rond-point du Bois-Rochin. Do you know the spot?"

"Yes, sire. I have fought there twice."

"What!" exclaimed the king, amazed at the reply [since dueling was illegal at the time].

"Under the edicts, sire, of Cardinal Richelieu," returned D'Artagnan, with his usual impassivity.

"That is very different, monsieur. You will therefore go there, and will examine the locality very carefully. A man has been wounded there, and you will find a horse lying dead. You will tell me what your opinion is upon the whole affair."

"Very good, sire."

"It is a matter of course that it is your own opinion I require, and not that of any one else."

"You shall have it in an hour's time, sire."

Without losing a second, D'Artagnan ran to the stable, took down the lantern, saddled his horse himself, and proceeded toward the place which his majesty had indicated. According to the promise he had made, he had neither seen nor met any one; and, he had carried his scruples so far as to do without the assistance of the helpers in the stables altogether. D'Artagnan was one of those who in moments of difficulty pride themselves on increasing their own value. By dint of hard galloping, he in less than five minutes reached the wood, fastened his horse to the first tree he came to, and penetrated to the broad open space on foot. He then began to inspect most carefully, on foot and with his lantern in his hand, the whole surface of the Rond-point, went forward, turned back again, measured, examined, and after half an hour's minute inspection, he returned silently to where he had left his horse, and pursued his way in deep reflection and at a foot-pace to Fontainebleau. Louis was waiting in his cabinet; he was alone, and with a pencil was scribbling on paper certain lines which D'Artagnan at first glance recognized as being very unequal and very much scratched about. The conclusion he arrived at was, that they must be verses. The king raised his head and perceived D'Artagnan.

"Well, monsieur," he said, "do you bring me any news?"

"Yes, sire."

"What have you seen?"

"As far as probability goes, sire," D'Artagnan began to reply.

"It was certainty I requested of you."

"I will approach it as near as I possibly can. The weather was very well adapted for investigations of the character I have just made; it has been raining this evening, and the roads were wet and muddy—"

"Well, the result, M. D'Artagnan?"

"Sire, your majesty told me that there was a horse lying dead in the cross-road of the Bois-Rochin, and I began, therefore, by studying the roads. I say the roads, because the center of the cross-road is reached by four separate roads. The one that I myself took was the only one that presented any fresh traces. Two horses had followed it side by side; their eight feet were marked very distinctly in the clay. One of the riders was more impatient than the other, for the footprints of the one were invariably in advance of the other about half a horse's length."

"Are you quite sure they came together?" said the king.

"Yes, sire. The horses are two rather large animals of equal pace—horses well used to maneuvers of all kinds, for they wheeled round the barrier of the Rond-point together."

"Well—and after?"

"The two cavaliers paused there for a moment, no doubt to arrange the conditions of the engagement; the horses grew restless and impatient. One of the riders spoke, while the other listened and seemed to have contented himself by simply answering. His horse pawed the ground, which proves that his attention was so taken up by listening that he let the bridle fall from his hand."

"A hostile meeting did take place, then?"

"Undoubtedly."

"Continue; you are a most accurate observer."

"One of the two cavaliers remained where he was standing, the one, in fact, who had been listening; the other crossed the open space, and at first placed himself directly opposite to his adversary. The one who had remained stationary traversed the Rond-point at a gallop, about two-thirds of its length, thinking that, by this means, he would gain upon his opponent; but the latter had followed the circumference of the wood."

"You are ignorant of their names, I suppose?"

"Completely so, sire. Only he who followed the circumference of the wood was mounted on a black horse."

"How do you know that?"

"I found a few hairs of his tail among the brambles which bordered the sides of the ditch."

"Go on."

"As for the other horse, there can be no trouble in describing him, since he was left dead on the field of battle."

"What was the cause of his death?"

"A ball which had passed through his temple."

"Was the ball that of a pistol or a gun?"

"It was a pistol-bullet, sire. Besides the manner in which the horse was wounded explained to me the tactics of the man who had killed it. He had followed the circumference of the wood in order to take his adversary in flank. Moreover, I followed his foot-tracks on the grass."

"The tracks of the black horse, do you mean?"

"Yes, sire."

"Go on, Monsieur D'Artagnan."

"As your majesty now perceives the position of the two adversaries, I will, for a moment, leave the cavalier who had remained stationary for the one who started off at a gallop."

"Do so."

"The horse of the cavalier who rode at full speed was killed on the spot."

"How do you know that?"

"The cavalier had not time even to throw himself off his horse, and so fell with it. I observed the impression of his leg, which with a great effort, he was enabled to extricate from under the horse. The spur, pressed down by the weight of the animal, had plowed up the ground."

"Very good; and what did he do as soon as he rose up again?"

"He walked straight up to his adversary."

"Who still remained upon the verge of the forest?"

"Yes, sire. Then, having reached a favorable distance, he stopped firmly, for the impression of both his heels are left in the ground quite close to each other, fired, and missed his adversary."

"How do you know he did not hit him?"

"I found a hat with a ball through it."

"Ah, a proof, then!" exclaimed the king.

"Insufficient, sire," replied D'Artagnan, coldly; "it is a hat without any letters indicating its ownership, without arms; a red feather, as all hats have; the lace, even, had nothing particular in it."

"Did the man with the hat through which the bullet had passed fire a second time?"

"Oh, sire, he had already fired twice."

"How did you ascertain that?"

"I found the waddings of the pistol."

"And what became of the bullet which did not kill the horse?"

"It cut in two the feather of the hat belonging to him against whom it was directed, and broke a small birch at the other end of the open glade."

"In that case, then, the man on the black horse was disarmed, while his adversary had still one more shot to fire."

"Sire, while the dismounted rider was extricating himself from his horse, the other was reloading his pistol. Only, he was much agitated while he was loading it, and his hand trembled greatly."

"How do you know that?"

"Half the charge fell to the ground, and he threw the ramrod aside, not having time to replace it in the pistol."

"Monsieur D'Artagnan, it is marvelous what you tell me."

"It is only close observation, sire, and the commonest highwayman would do as much."

"The whole scene is before me from the manner in which you relate it."

"I have, in fact, reconstructed it in my own mind, with merely a few alterations."

"And now," said the king, "let us return to the dismounted cavalier. You were saying that he had walked toward his adversary while the latter was loading his pistol."

"Yes; but at the very moment he himself was taking aim, the other fired."

"Oh!" said the king; "and the shot?"

"The shot told terribly, sire; the dismounted cavalier fell upon his face, after having staggered forward three or four paces."

"Where was he hit?"

"In two places; in the first place, in his right hand, and then, by the same bullet, in his chest."

"But how could you ascertain that?" inquired the king, full of admiration.

"By a very simple means; the butt-end of the pistol was covered with blood, and the trace of the bullet could be observed with fragments of a broken ring. The wounded man, in all probability, had the ring-finger and the little finger carried off."

"As far as the hand goes, I have nothing to say; but the chest!"

"Sire, there were two small pools of blood, at a distance of about two feet and a half from each other. At one of these pools of blood the grass was torn up by the clenched hand; at the other the grass was simply pressed down by the weight of the body."

"Poor De Guiche!" exclaimed the king.

"Ah! it was M. de Guiche, then?" said the musketeer, very quietly. "I suspected it, but did not venture to mention it to your majesty."

"And what made you suspect it?"

"I recognized the De Grammont arms upon the holsters of the dead horse."

"And you think he is seriously wounded?"

"Very seriously, since he fell immediately, and remained a long time in the same place; however, he was able to walk, as he left the spot, supported by two friends."

"You met him returning, then?"

"No; but I observed the foot-prints of three men; the one on the right and the one on the left walked freely and easily, but the one in the middle dragged his feet as he walked; besides, he left traces of blood at every step he took."

"Now, monsieur, since you saw the combat so distinctly that not a single detail seems to have escaped you, tell me something about De Guiche's adversary?"

"Oh, sire, I do not know him."

"And yet you see everything very clearly."

"Yes, sire, I see everything; but I do not tell all I see; and, since the poor devil has escaped, your majesty will permit me to say that I do not intend to denounce him."

"And yet he is guilty, since he has fought a duel, monsieur."

"Not guilty in my eyes, sire," said D'Artagnan, coldly.

"Monsieur!" exclaimed the king, "are you aware of what you are saying?"

"Perfectly, sire; but, according to any notion, a man who fights a duel is a brave man; such, at least, is my own opinion; but your majesty may have another; that is very natural—you are the master here."

"Monsieur D'Artagnan, I ordered you, however—"

D'Artagnan interrupted the king, by a respectful gesture. "You ordered me, sire, to gather what particulars I could, respecting a hostile meeting that had taken place; those particulars you have. If you order me to arrest M. de Guiche's adversary, I will do so; but do not order me to denounce him to you, for in that case I will not obey."

"Very well! Arrest him, then."

"Give me his name, sire."

The king stamped his foot angrily; but after a moment's reflection, he said, "You are right—ten times, twenty times, a hundred times right."

"That is my opinion, sire; I am happy that, this time, it accords with your majesty's."

"One word more. Who assisted De Guiche?"

"I do not know, sire."

"But you speak of two men. There was a person present, then, as second."

"There was no second, sire. Nay, more than that, when M. de Guiche fell, his adversary fled without giving him any assistance."

"The miserable coward!" exclaimed the king.

"The consequence of your ordinances, sire. If a man has already escaped one chance of death, he naturally wishes to escape a second. M. de Botteville cannot be forgotten very easily."

"And so, men turn cowards."

"No, they become prudent."

"And he has fled, then, you say?"

"Yes; and as fast as his horse could possibly carry him."

"In what direction?"

"In the direction of the château."

"Well; and after—?"

"Afterward, as I have had the honor of telling your majesty, two men on foot arrived, who carried M. de Guiche back with them."

"What proof have you that these men arrived after the combat?"

"A very evident proof, sire; at the moment the encounter took place, the rain had just ceased, the ground had not had time to imbibe the moisture, and had, consequently, become damp; the footsteps sunk in the ground; but, while M. de Guiche was lying there in a fainting condition the ground became firm again, and the footsteps made a less sensible impression."

Louis clapped his hands together in sign of admiration. "Monsieur D'Artagnan," he said, "you are positively the cleverest man in my kingdom."

"The very thing that M. de Richelieu thought, and M. de Mazarin said, sire."

"And now it remains for us to see if your sagacity is in fault."

"Oh! sire, a man may be mistaken; *errare humanum est*," said the musketeer, philosophically.

"In that case, you are not human, Monsieur D'Artagnan, for I believe you never are mistaken."

"Your majesty said that we were going to see whether such was the case or not."

"Yes."

"In what way, may I venture to ask?"

"I have sent for M. de Manicamp, and M. de Manicamp is coming."

"And M. de Manicamp knows the secret?"

"Guiche has no secrets from M. de Manicamp."

D'Artagnan shook his head. "No one was present at the combat, I repeat; and, unless M. de Manicamp was one of the two men who brought him back—"

"Hush!" said the king, "he is coming; remain there, and listen attentively."

"Very good, sire."

And, at the same moment, Manicamp and Saint-Aignan appeared at the threshold of the door.

The king with his hand made, first to the musketeer, and then to Saint-Aignan, an imperious and significant gesture, as much as to say, "On your lives, not a word." D'Artagnan withdrew like a soldier into a corner of the room; Saint-Aignan, in his character of favorite, leaned over the back of the king's chair. Manicamp, with his right foot properly advanced, a smile upon his lips, and his white and well-formed hands gracefully disposed, advanced to make his reverence to the king, who returned the salutation by a bow.

"Good evening, M. de Manicamp," he said.

"Your majesty did me the honor to send for me," said Manicamp.

"Yes, in order to learn from you all the details of the unfortunate accident which has befallen the Comte de Guiche."

"Oh! sire, it is very grievous indeed."

"You were there?"

"Not precisely so, sire."

"But you arrived on the scene where the accident occurred a few minutes after it took place?"

"I did so, sire, about half an hour afterward."

"And where did the accident happen?"

"I believe, sire, the place is called the Rond-point du Bois-Rochin."

"Oh! the rendezvous of the hunt."

"The very spot, sire."

"Very good; tell me what details you are acquainted with respecting this unhappy affair, Monsieur de Manicamp."

"Perhaps your majesty has already been informed of them, and I fear to fatigue you by useless repetitions."

"No, do not be afraid of that."

Manicamp looked all around him; he only saw D'Artagnan leaning with his back against the wainscot—D'Artagnan, calm, kind, and good-natured as usual—and Saint-Aignan whom he had accompanied, and who still leaned over the king's armchair with an expression of countenance equally full of good feeling. He determined, therefore, to speak out. "Your majesty is perfectly aware," he said, "that accidents are very frequent in hunting."

"In hunting, do you say?"

"I mean, sire, when an animal is brought to bay."

"Ah! ah!" said the king, "it was when the animal was brought to bay, then, that the accident happened."

"Alas! sire, unhappily, it was so."

The king paused for a moment before he said: "What animal was being hunted?"

"A wild boar, sire."

"And what could possibly have possessed De Guiche to go to a wild-boar hunt by himself; that is but a clownish idea of sport, and only fit for that class of people who, unlike the Marechal de Grammont, have no dogs and huntsmen to hunt as gentlemen should do."

Manicamp shrugged his shoulders. "Youth is very rash," he said sententiously.

"Well, go on," said the king.

"At all events," continued Manicamp, not venturing to be too precipitate and hasty, and letting his words fall very slowly, one by one, "at all events, sire, poor De Guiche went hunting—quite alone."

"Quite alone, indeed! What a sportsman. And is not M. de Guiche aware that the wild boar always stands at bay?"

"That is the very thing that really happened, sire."

"He had some idea, then, of the beast being there?"

"Yes, sire, some peasants had seen it among their potatoes."

"And what kind of animal was it?"

"A short, thick beast."

"You may as well tell me, monsieur, that Guiche had some idea of committing suicide, for I have seen him hunt, and he is an active and vigorous hunter. Whenever he fires at an animal brought to bay and held in check by the dogs, he takes every possible precaution, and yet he fires with a carbine, and on this occasion he seems to have faced the boar with pistols only."

Manicamp started.

"A costly pair of pistols, excellent weapons to fight a duel with a man and not with a wild boar. What absurdity."

"There are some things, sire, which are difficult of explanation."

"You are quite right, and the event which we are now discussing is one of those things. Go on."

During the recital, Saint-Aignan, who had probably made a sign to Manicamp to be careful what he was about, found that the king's glance was constantly fixed upon himself, so that it was utterly impossible to communicate with Manicamp in any way. As for D'Artagnan, the statue of Silence at Athens was far more noisy and far more expressive than he. Manicamp, therefore, was obliged to continue in the same way he had begun, and so contrived to get more and more entangled in his explanation. "Sire," he said, "this is probably how the affair happened. Guiche was waiting to receive the boar as it rushed toward him."

"On foot or on horseback?" inquired the king.

"On horseback. He fired upon the brute and missed his aim, and then it dashed upon him."

"And the horse was killed?"

"Ah! your majesty knows that, then."

"I have been told that a horse has been found lying dead in the crossroads of the Bois-Rochin, and I presume it was De Guiche's horse."

"Perfectly true, sire, it was his."

"Well, so much for the horse, now for De Guiche?"

"Guiche, once down, was attacked and worried by the wild boar, and wounded in the hand and in the chest."

"It is a horrible accident, but it must be admitted it was De Guiche's own fault. How could he possibly have gone to hunt such an animal merely armed with pistols; he must have forgotten the fable of Adonis?"

Manicamp rubbed his ear in seeming perplexity. "Very true," he said, "it was very imprudent."

"Can you explain it, Monsieur Manicamp?"

"Sire, what is written is written!"

"Ah! you are a fatalist."

Manicamp looked very uncomfortable and ill at ease.

"I am angry with you, Monsieur Manicamp," continued the king.

"With me, sire?"

"Yes. How was it that you, who are De Guiche's intimate friend, and who knows that he is subject to such acts of folly, did not stop him in time?"

Manicamp hardly knew what to do; the tone in which the king spoke was not exactly that of a credulous man. On the other hand, the tone did not indicate any particular severity, nor did he seem to care very much about the cross-examination. There was more of raillery in it than of menace.

"And you say, then," continued the king, "that it was positively De Guiche's horse that was found dead?"

"Quite positive, sire."

"Did that astonish you?"

"No, sire: for your majesty will remember that, at the last hunt, M. de Saint-Maure had a horse killed under him, and in the same way."

"Yes, but that one was ripped open."

"Of course, sire."

"Had Guiche's horse been ripped open, like M. de Saint-Maure's horse, that would not have astonished me, indeed."

Manicamp opened his eyes very wide.

"Am I mistaken," resumed the king, "was it not in the temple that De Guiche's horse was struck? You must admit, Monsieur de Manicamp, that that is a very singular wound."

"You are aware, sire, that the horse is a very intelligent animal, and he endeavored to defend himself."

"But a horse defends himself with his hind feet, and not with his head."

"In that case the terrified horse might have slipped or fallen down," said Manicamp, "and the boar, you understand, sire, the boar—"

"Oh! I understand that perfectly, as far as the horse is concerned; but how about his rider?"

"Well! that, too, is simple enough; the boar left the horse and attacked the rider; and, as I have already had the honor of informing your majesty, shattered De Guiche's hand at the very moment he was about to discharge the second pistol at him, and then, with a blow of his tusk, made that terrible hole in his chest."

"Nothing can possibly be more likely; really, Monsieur de Manicamp, you are wrong in placing so little confidence in your own eloquence, and you can tell a story most admirably."

"Your majesty is exceedingly kind," said Manicamp, saluting him in the most embarrassed manner.

"From this day henceforth, I will prohibit any gentleman attached to my court going to a similar encounter. Really, one might just as well permit dueling."

Manicamp started, and moved as if he were about to withdraw. "Is your majesty satisfied?" he inquired.

"Delighted; but do not withdraw yet, Monsieur de Manicamp," said Louis, "I have something to say to you."

"Well, well!" thought D'Artagnan, "there is another who is not up to our mark;" and he uttered a sigh which might signify, "Oh! the men of our stamp, where are they now?"

At this moment an usher lifted up the curtain before the door, and announced the king's physician.

"Ah!" exclaimed Louis, "here comes Monsieur Valot, who has just been to see M. de Guiche. We shall now hear news of the wounded man."

Manicamp felt more uncomfortable than ever.

"In this way, at least," added the king, "our conscience will be quite clear." And he looked at D'Artagnan, who did not seem in the slightest degree discomposed.

M. Valot entered. The position of the different persons present was precisely the same: the king was seated, Saint-Aignan still leaning over the back of his armchair, D'Artagnan with his back against the wall, and Manicamp still standing.

"Well, M. Valot," said the king, "have you obeyed my directions?"

"With the greatest alacrity, sire."

"You went to the doctor's house in Fontainebleau?"

"Yes, sire."

"And you found M. de Guiche there?"

"I did, sire."

"What state was he in? Speak unreservedly."

"In a very sad state, indeed, sire."

"The wild boar did not quite devour him, however?"

"Devour whom?"

"Guiche."

"What wild boar?"

"The boar that wounded him."

"M. de Guiche wounded by a boar?"

"So it is said, at least."

"By a poacher, rather, or by a jealous husband, or an ill-used lover, who, in order to be revenged, fired upon him."

"What is that you say, Monsieur Valot? Are not M. de Guiche's wounds produced by defending himself against a wild boar?"

"M. de Guiche's wounds are produced by a pistol-bullet which broke his ring-finger and the little finger of the right hand, and afterward buried itself in the intercostal muscles of the chest."

"A bullet! Are you sure Monsieur de Guiche has been wounded

by a bullet?" exclaimed the king, pretending to look much surprised.

"Indeed I am, sire; so sure, in fact, that here it is." And he presented to the king a half-flattened bullet, which the king looked at, but did not touch.

"Did he have that in his chest, poor fellow?" he asked.

"Not precisely. The ball did not penetrate, but was flattened, as you see, either upon the trigger of the pistol or upon the right side of the breast-bone."

"Good heavens!" said the king, seriously, "you said nothing to me about this, Monsieur de Manicamp."

"Sire—"

"What does all this mean, then—this invention about hunting a wild boar at nightfall? Come, speak, monsieur."

"Sire—"

"It seems, then, that you are right," said the king, turning round toward his captain of musketeers, "and that a duel actually took place."

The king possessed, to a greater extent than any one else, the faculty enjoyed by the great in power or position, of compromising and dividing those beneath him. Manicamp darted a look full of reproaches at the musketeer. D'Artagnan understood the look at once, and, not wishing to remain beneath the weight of such an accusation, advanced a step forward, and said: "Sire, your majesty commanded me to go and explore the place where the crossroads meet in the Bois-Rochin, and to report to you, according to my own ideas, what had taken place there. I submitted my observations to you, but without denouncing any one. It was your majesty yourself who was the first to name the Comte de Guiche."

"Well, monsieur, well," said the king, haughtily, "you have done your duty, and I am satisfied with you. But you, Monsieur de Manicamp, have failed in yours, for you have told me a falsehood."

"A falsehood, sire. The expression is a hard one."

"Find another instead, then."

"Sire, I will not attempt to do so. I have already been unfortunate enough to displease your majesty, and it will, in every respect, be far better for me to accept most humbly any reproaches you may think proper to address to me."

"You are right, monsieur; whoever conceals the truth from me risks my displeasure."

"Sometimes, sire, one is ignorant of the truth."

"No further falsehood, monsieur, or I double the punishment."

Manicamp bowed and turned pale. D'Artagnan again made another step forward, determined to interfere, if the still increasing anger of the king attained certain limits.

"You see, monsieur," continued the king, "that it is useless to deny the thing any longer. M. de Guiche has fought a duel."

"I do not deny it, sire; and it would have been generous in your majesty not to have forced me to tell a falsehood."

"Forced! Who forced you?"

"Sire, M. de Guiche is my friend: your majesty has forbidden duels under pain of death; a falsehood might save my friend's life, and I told it."

"Good!" murmured D'Artagnan, "an excellent fellow, upon my word."

"Instead of telling a falsehood, monsieur, you should have prevented him from fighting," said the king.

"Oh, sire, your majesty, who is the most accomplished gentleman in France, knows quite as well as any of us other gentlemen that we have never considered M. de Botteville dishonored for having suffered death on the Place de Grève. That which does in truth dishonor a man is to avoid meeting his enemy, and not to avoid meeting his executioner."

"Well, monsieur, that may be so," said Louis XIV. "I am very desirous of suggesting a means of your repairing all."

"If it be a means of which a gentleman may avail himself, I shall most eagerly do so."

"The name of M. de Guiche's adversary?"

"Oh, oh!" murmured D'Artagnan, "are we going to take Louis XIII as a model?"

"Sire!" said Manicamp, with an accent of reproach.

"You will not name him, it appears, then?" said the king.

"Sire, I do not know him."

"Bravo!" murmured D'Artagnan.

"Monsieur de Manicamp, hand your sword to the captain."

Manicamp bowed very gracefully, unbuckled his sword, smiling as he did so, and handed it for the musketeer to take. But Saint-Aignan advanced hurriedly between him and D'Artagnan.

"Sire," he said, "will your majesty permit me to say a word?"

"Do so," said the king, delighted perhaps at the bottom of his heart for some one to step between him and the wrath which he felt had carried him too far.

"Manicamp, you are a brave man, and the king will appreciate your conduct; but to wish to serve your friends too well is to destroy them. Manicamp, you know the name the king asks you for?"

"It is perfectly true—I do know it."

"You will give it up then?"

"If I felt I ought to have mentioned it, I should have already done so."

"Then I will tell it, for I am not so extremely sensitive on such points of honor as you are."

"You are at liberty to do so, but it seems to me, however—"

"Oh! a truce to magnanimity; I will not permit you to go to the Bastille in that way. Do you speak; or I will."

Manicamp was keen-witted enough, and perfectly understood that he had done quite sufficient to produce a good opinion of his conduct; it was now only a question of persevering in such a manner as to regain the good graces of the king.

"Speak, monsieur," he said to Saint-Aignan; "I have on my own behalf done all that my conscience told me to do, and it must have been very importunate," he added, turning toward the king, "since its mandates led me to disobey your majesty's commands; but your majesty will forgive me, I hope, when you learn that I was anxious to preserve the honor of a lady."

"Of a lady?" said the king, with some uneasiness.

"Yes, sire."

"A lady was the cause of this duel?"

Manicamp bowed.

"If the position of the lady in question warrants it," he said, "I shall not complain of your having acted with so much circum-spection; on the contrary, indeed."

"Sire, everything which concerns your majesty's household, or the household of your majesty's brother, is of importance in my eyes."

"In my brother's household," repeated Louis XIV with a slight hesitation. "The cause of the duel was a lady belonging to my brother's household, do you say?"

"Or to Madame's."

"Ah! to Madame's?"

"Yes, sire."

"Well—and this lady?"

"Is one of the maids of honor of her royal highness, Madame la Duchesse d'Orleans."

"For whom M. de Guiche fought—do you say?"

"Yes, sire, and, this time, I tell no falsehood."

Louis seemed restless and anxious. "Gentlemen," he said, turning toward the spectators of this scene, "will you have the goodness to retire for a moment? I wish to be alone with M. de Manicamp; I know he has some very important communications to make for his own justification, and which he will not venture to do before witness....Put up your sword, Monsieur de Manicamp."

Manicamp returned his sword to his belt.

"The fellow decidedly has his wits about him," murmured the musketeer, taking Saint-Aignan by the arm, and withdrawing with him.

"He will get out of it," said the latter in D'Artagnan's ear.

"And with honor, too, Comte."

Manicamp cast a glance of acknowledgment at Saint-Aignan and the captain, which passed unnoticed by the king.

"Come, come," said D'Artagnan, as he left the room, "I had an indifferent opinion of the new generation. Well, I was mistaken after all, and there is some good in them, I perceive."

Valot preceded the favorite and the captain, leaving the king and Manicamp alone in the cabinet.

Determined to be satisfied that no one was listening, the king went himself to the door, and then returned precipitously and placed himself opposite to Manicamp. "And now we are alone, Monsieur de Manicamp, explain yourself?"

"With the greatest frankness, sire," replied the young man.

"And, in the first place, pray understand," added the king, "that there is nothing to which I personally attach a greater importance than the honor of any lady."

"That is the very reason, sire, why I endeavored to study your delicacy of sentiment and feeling."

"Yes, I understand it all now. You say that it was one of the maids of honor of my sister-in-law who was the subject of dispute, and that the person in question, Guiche's adversary, the man, in point of fact, whom you will not name—"

"But whom M. de Saint-Aignan will name, monsieur."

"Yes; you say, however, that this man has insulted some one belonging to the household of Madame."

"Yes, sire, Mademoiselle de la Vallière."

"Ah!" said the king, as if he had expected the name, and yet as if its announcement had caused him a sudden pang; "ah! it was Mademoiselle de la Vallière who was insulted."

"I do not say precisely that she was insulted, sire."

"But at all events—"

"I merely say that she was spoken of in terms far from respectful."

"A man dares to speak in disrespectful terms of Mademoiselle de la Vallière, and yet you refuse to tell me the name of the insulter."

"Sire, I thought it was quite understood that your majesty had abandoned the idea of making me denounce him."

"Perfectly true, monsieur," returned the king, controlling his anger; "besides, I shall always know in sufficient time the name of the man whom I shall feel it my duty to punish."

Manicamp perceived that they had returned to the question again. As for the king, he saw he had allowed himself to be hurried away a little too far, and he therefore continued:

"And I will punish him—not because there is any question of Mademoiselle de la Vallière, although I esteem her very highly—but because a lady was the object of the quarrel. And I intend that ladies shall be respected at my court, and that quarrels shall be put a stop to altogether."

Manicamp bowed.

"And now, Monsieur de Manicamp," continued the king, "what was said about Mademoiselle de la Vallière?"

"Cannot your majesty guess?"

"I?"

"Your majesty can imagine the character of the jests in which young men permit themselves to indulge."

"They very probably said that she was in love with some one?" the king ventured to remark.

"Probably so."

"But Mademoiselle de la Vallière has a perfect right to love any one she pleases," said the king.

"That is the very point De Guiche maintained."

"And on account of which he fought, do you mean?"

"Yes sire, the very sole cause."

The king colored. "And you do not know anything more, then?"

"In what respect, sire?"

"In the very interesting respect which you are now referring to."

"What does your majesty wish to know?"

"Why, the name of the man with whom La Vallière is in love, and whom De Guiche's adversary disputed her right to love."

"Sire, I know nothing—I have heard nothing—and have learned nothing, even accidentally; but De Guiche is a noble-hearted fellow, and if, momentarily, he substituted himself in the place or stead of La Vallière's protector, it was because that protector was himself of too exalted a position to undertake her defense."

These words were more than transparent; they made the king blush, but this time with pleasure. He struck Manicamp gently on the shoulder.

"Well, well, Monsieur de Manicamp, you are not only a ready, witty fellow, but a brave gentleman besides, and your friend De Guiche is a paladin quite after my own heart; you will express that to him for me."

"Your majesty forgives me, then?"

"Completely."

"And I am free?"

The king smiled and held out his hand to Manicamp, which he took and kissed respectfully.

"And then," added the king, "you relate stories so charmingly."

"I, sire?"

"You told me in the most admirable manner the particulars of the accident which happened to Guiche. I can see the wild boar rushing out of the wood—I can see the horse fall down, and the boar rush from the horse to the rider. You do not simply relate a story well, but you positively paint its incidents."

"Sire, I think your majesty deigns to laugh at my expense."

"On the contrary," said Louis, seriously, "I have so little intention of laughing, Monsieur de Manicamp, that I wish you to relate this adventure to every one."

"The adventure of the hunt?"

"Yes; in the same manner you told it to me, without changing a single word—you understand."

"Perfectly, sire."

"And you will relate it, then?"

"Without losing a minute."

"Very well! and now summon M. D'Artagnan; I hope you are no longer afraid of him."

"Oh! sire, from the very moment I am sure of your majesty's kind dispositions, I no longer fear anything!"

"Call him, then," said the king.

Manicamp opened the door, and said, "Gentlemen, the king wishes you to return." D'Artagnan, Saint-Aignan and Valot entered.

"Gentlemen," said the king, "I summoned you for the purpose of saying that Monsieur de Manicamp's explanation has entirely satisfied me."

D'Artagnan glanced at Valot and Saint-Aignan, as much as to say, "Well! did I not tell you so?"

The king led Manicamp to the door, and then in a low tone of voice, said, "See that M. de Guiche takes good care of himself, and, particularly that he recovers as soon as possible; I am very desirous of thanking him in the name of every lady, but let him take special care that he does not begin again."

"Were he to die a hundred times, sire, he would begin again if your majesty's honor were in any way called into question."

This remark was direct enough. But we have already said that the incense of flattery was very pleasing to the king, and, provided he received it, he was not very particular as to its quality.

"Very well, very well," he said, as he dismissed Manicamp, "I will see De Guiche myself, and make him listen to reason." And as Manicamp left the apartment, the king turned round toward the three spectators of this scene, and said, "Tell me, Monsieur D'Argagnan, how does it happen that your sight is so imperfect?—you, whose eyes are generally so very good."

"My sight bad, sire?"

"Certainly."

"It must be the case, since your majesty says so; but in what respect, may I ask?"

"Why, with regard to what occurred in the Bois-Rochin."

"Ah! ah!"

"Certainly. You pretend to have seen the tracks of two horses, to have detected the foot-prints of two men; and have described the particulars of an engagement, which you assert took place. Nothing of the sort occurred; pure illusion on your part."

"Ah! ah!" said D'Artagnan.

"Exactly the same thing with the galloping to and fro of the horses, and the other indications of a struggle. It was the struggle of De Guiche against the wild boar, and absolutely nothing else; only the struggle was a long and a terrible one, it seems."

"Ah! ah!" continued D'Artagnan.

"And when I think that I almost believed it for a moment; but, then, you speak with such confidence."

"I admit, sire, that I must have been very short-sighted," said D'Artagnan, with a readiness of humor which delighted the king.

"You do admit, then?"

"Admit it, sire, most assuredly I do."

"So that now you see the thing—"

"In quite a different light to what I saw it half an hour ago."

"And to what, then, do you attribute this difference in your opinion?"

"Oh! a very simple thing, sire; half an hour ago I returned from the Bois-Rochin, where I had nothing to light me but a stupid stable lantern—"

"While now?"

"While now, I have all the wax-lights of your cabinet, and more than that, your majesty's own eyes, which illuminate everything, like the blazing sun at noonday."

The king began to laugh, and Saint-Aignan broke out into loud convulsions of merriment.

"It is precisely like M. Valot," said D'Artagnan, resuming the conversation where the king had left off; "he has been imagining all along, that, not only was M. de Guiche wounded by a bullet, but still more, that he extracted it even from his chest."

"Upon my word," said Valot, "I assure you—"

"Now, did you not believe that?" continued D'Artagnan.

"Yes," said Valot, "not only did I believe it, but at this very moment I would swear it."

"Well, my dear doctor, you have dreamed it."

"I have dreamed it!"

"M. de Guiche's wound—a mere dream; the bullet a dream. So take my advice, and say no more about it."

"Well said," returned the king; "M. D'Artagnan's advice is very good. Do not speak of your dream to any one, M. Valot, and upon the word of a gentleman, you will have no occasion to repent it. Good evening, gentlemen; a very sad affair indeed is a wild-boar hunt!"

"A very serious thing indeed," repeated D'Artagnan, in a loud voice, "is a wild-boar hunt!" and he repeated it in every room through which he passed, and left the château, taking Valot with him.

"And now we are alone," said the king to Saint-Aignan, "what is the name of De Guiche's adversary?" Saint-Aignan looked at the king.

"Oh! do not hesitate," said the king; "you know that I must forgive."

"De Wardes," said Saint-Aignan.

"Very good," said Louis XIV, and then hastily retiring to his own room, added to himself, "To forgive is not to forget."

A Touch
of the Continental

From *Bleak House*

CHARLES DICKENS

Charles Dickens (1812–1870) used *Bleak House* (1853) to attack the legal system of his time, its delays, its injustices, its attendant evils. Yet buried in this novel of social protest lies a tightly constructed murder plot, complete with police detective, innocent suspect, and clever killer. But Dickens goes at it all backwards, to the modern way of thinking, by letting "Inspector Bucket of the Detective" solve the murder offstage, and then *explain* it onstage. However, as this excerpt shows, one of the most important elements of the detective-genre-to-come is the wrap-up explanation of the chain of deduction that leads to the solution. Dickens clearly understands the use of clues, hard evidence—even today's "smoking gun" appears in an earlier incarnation—in his wrap-up. Note that some eighty years before Dashiell Hammett popularizes Nick and Nora Charles as a husband-and-wife detective team (*The Thin Man*, 1934), Dickens clearly establishes a similar team in Mr. and Mrs. Bucket!

The scene in this excerpt from *Bleak House* takes place in the study of Sir Leicester Dedlock's mansion. Mr. Tulkinghorn, a wily, slick, reprehensible attorney, has been murdered and Bucket is about to tell the Baronet how he has wrapped up the case. Let the modern reader not be thrown off by the use of the historical present tense; Dickens was always experimenting with style.

135

"Sir Leicester Dedlock, Baronet, I mentioned yesterday evening that I wanted but a very little to complete this case. I have now completed it and collected proof against the person who did this crime."

Sir Leicester looks astounded and inquires, "Is the man in custody?"

Mr. Bucket tells him, after a pause, "It was a woman."

Sir Leicester leans back in his chair, and breathlessly ejaculates, "Good heaven!"

"The party to be apprehended is now in this house, and I'm about to take her into custody in your presence. Sir Leicester Dedlock, Baronet, don't you say a word nor yet stir. There'll be no noise and no disturbance at all. Don't you be nervous on account of the apprehension at present coming off. You shall see the whole case clear, from first to last."

Mr. Bucket rings, goes to the door, briefly whispers, shuts the door, and stands behind it with his arms folded. After a suspense of a minute or two the door slowly opens and a Frenchwoman enters. Mademoiselle Hortense.

The moment she is in the room Mr. Bucket claps the door to and puts his back against it. The suddenness of the noise occasions her to turn, and then for the first time she sees Sir Leicester Dedlock in his chair.

"I ask your pardon," she mutters hurriedly. "They tell me there was no one here."

Her step towards the door brings her front to front with Mr. Bucket. Suddenly a spasm shoots across her face and she turns deadly pale.

"This is my lodger, Sir Leicester Dedlock," says Mr. Bucket, nodding at her. "This foreign young woman has been my lodger for some weeks back."

"What do Sir Leicester care for that, you think, my angel?" returns mademoiselle in a jocular strain.

"Why, my angel," returns Mr. Bucket, "we shall see."

Mademoiselle Hortense eyes him with a scowl upon her tight face, which gradually changes into a smile of scorn. "You are very mysterieuse. Are you drunk?"

"Tolerable sober, my angel," returns Mr. Bucket.

"I come from arriving at this so detestable house with your wife. Your wife have left me since some minutes. They tell me downstairs that your wife is here. I come here, and your wife is not here. What is the intention of this fool's play, say then?" mademoiselle demands, with her arms composedly crossed, but with something in her dark cheek beating like a clock.

Mr. Bucket merely shakes the finger at her.

"Ah, my God, you are an unhappy idiot!" cries mademoiselle with a toss of her head and a laugh. "Leave me to pass downstairs, great pig." With a stamp of her foot and a menace.

"Now, mademoiselle," says Mr. Bucket in a cool determined way, "you go and sit down upon that sofy."

"I will not sit down upon nothing," she replies with a shower of nods.

"Now, mademoiselle," repeats Mr. Bucket, making no demonstration except with the finger, "you sit down upon that sofy."

"Why?"

"Because I take you into custody on a charge of murder, and you don't need to be told it. Now, I want to be polite to one of your sex and a foreigner if I can. If I can't, I must be rough, and there's rougher ones outside. What I am to be depends on you. So I recommend you, as a friend, afore another half a blessed moment has passed over your head, to go and sit down upon that sofy."

Mademoiselle complies, saying in a concentrated while that something in her cheek beats fast and hard, "You are a devil."

"Now, you see," Mr. Bucket proceeds approvingly, "you're comfortable and conducting yourself as I should expect a foreign young woman of your sense to do. So I'll give you a piece of advice, and it's this, don't you talk too much. You're not expected to say anything here, and you can't keep too quiet a tongue in your head. In short, the less you *parlay*, the better, you know." Mr. Bucket is very complacent over this French explanation.

Mademoiselle, with that tigerish expansion of the mouth and her black eyes darting fire upon him, sits upright on the sofa in a rigid state, with her hands clenched—and her feet too, one might suppose—muttering, "Oh, you Bucket, you are a devil!"

"Now, Sir Leicester Dedlock, Baronet," says Mr. Bucket, and from this time forth the finger never rests, "this young woman, my lodger, was her ladyship's maid at the time I have mentioned to you; and this young woman, besides being extraordinary vehement and passionate against her ladyship after being discharged—"

"Lies!" cries mademoiselle. "I discharge myself."

"Now, why don't you take my advice?" returns Mr. Bucket in an impressive, almost in an imploring, tone. "I'm surprised at the indiscreetness you commit. You'll say something that'll be used against you, you know. You're sure to come to it. Never you mind what I say till it's given in evidence. It is not addressed to you."

"Discharge, too," cries mademoiselle furiously, "by her lady-ship! Eh, my faith, a pretty ladyship! Why, I r-r-r-ruin my character by remaining with a ladyship so infame!"

"Upon my soul I wonder at you!" Mr. Bucket remonstrates. "I thought the French were a polite nation, I did, really. Yet to hear a female going on like that before Sir Leicester Dedlock, Baronet!"

"He is a poor abused!" cries mademoiselle. "I spit upon his house, upon his name, upon his imbecility," all of which she makes the carpet represent. "Oh, that he is a great man! Oh, yes, superb! Oh, heaven! Bah!"

"Well, Sir Leicester Dedlock," proceeds Mr. Bucket, "this intemperate foreigner also angrily took it into her head that she had established a claim upon Mr. Tulkinghorn, deceased, though she was liberally paid for her time and trouble."

"Lies!" cries mademoiselle. "I ref-use his money all togezzer."

"If you *will parlay*, you know," says Mr. Bucket parentheti-cally, "you must take the consequences. Now, whether she became my lodger, Sir Leicester Dedlock, with any deliberate intention then of doing this deed and blinding me, I give no opinion on; but she lived in my house in that capacity at the time that she was hovering about the chambers of the deceased Mr. Tulkinghorn with a view to a wrangle."

"Lie!" cries mademoiselle. "All lie!"

"The murder was committed, Sir Leicester Dedlock, Baronet, and you know under what circumstances. [Tulkinghorn was shot to death with a pistol.] Now, I beg of you to follow me close with your attention for a minute or two. I was sent for, and the case was entrusted to me. I examined the place, and the body, and the papers, and everything. From information I received (from a clerk in the same house) I took [Mr.] George into custody as having been seen hanging about there on the night, and at very nigh the time of the murder, also as having been overheard in high words with the deceased on former occasions—even threatening him, as the witness made out. If you ask me, Sir Leicester Dedlock, whether from the first I believed George to be the murderer, I tell you candidly no, but he might be, notwithstanding, and there was enough against him to make it my duty to take him and get him kept under remand. Now, observe!"

As Mr. Bucket bends forward in some excitement—for him—and inaugurates what he is going to say with one ghostly beat of his forefinger in the air, Mademoiselle Hortense fixes her black eyes upon him with a dark frown and sets her dry lips closely and firmly together.

"I went home, Sir Leicester Dedlock, Baronet, at night and found this young woman having supper with my wife, Mrs. Bucket. She had made a mighty show of being fond of Mrs. Bucket from her first offering herself as our lodger, but that night she made more than ever—in fact, overdid it. Likewise she overdid her respect, and all that, for the lamented memory of the deceased Mr. Tulkinghorn. By the living Lord it flashed upon me, as I sat opposite to her at the table and saw her with a knife in her hand, that she had done it!"

Mademoiselle is hardly audible in straining through her teeth and lips the words, "You are a devil."

"Now where," pursues Mr. Bucket, "had she been on the night of the murder? She had been to the theayter. (She really was there, I have since found, both before the deed and after it.) I knew I had an artful customer to deal with and that proof would be very difficult; and I laid a trap for her—such a trap as I never laid yet, and such a venture as I never made yet. I worked it out in my mind while I was talking to her at supper. When I went upstairs to bed, our house being small and this young woman's ears sharp, I stuffed the sheet into Mrs. Bucket's mouth that she shouldn't say a word of surprise and told her all about it. My dear, don't you give your mind to that again, or I shall link your feet together at the ankles." Mr. Bucket, breaking off, has made a noiseless descent upon mademoiselle and laid his heavy hand upon her shoulder.

"What is the matter with you now?" she asks him.

"Don't you think any more," returns Mr. Bucket with admonitory finger, "of throwing yourself out of window. That's what's the matter with me. Come! Just take my arm. You needn't get up; I'll sit down by you. Now take my arm, will you? I'm a married man, you know; you're acquainted with my wife. Just take my arm."

Vainly endeavouring to moisten those dry lips, with a painful sound she struggles with herself and complies.

"Now we're all right again. Sir Leicester Dedlock, Baronet, this case could never have been the case it is but for Mrs. Bucket, who is a woman in fifty thousand—in a hundred and fifty thousand! To throw this young woman off her guard, I have never set foot in our house since, though I've communicated with Mrs. Bucket in the baker's loaves and in the milk as often as required. My whispered words to Mrs. Bucket when she had the sheet in her mouth were, 'My dear, can you throw her off continually with natural accounts of my suspicions against George, and this, and that, and t'other? Can you do without rest and keep watch upon her night and day? Can you undertake to say, "She shall do nothing without my knowledge, she shall be my prisoner without suspecting it, she shall no more escape from me than from death, and her life shall be my life, and her soul my soul, till I have got her, if she did this murder?"' Mrs. Bucket says to me, as well as she could speak on account of the sheet, 'Bucket, I can!' And she has acted up to it glorious!"

"Lies!" mademoiselle interposes. "All lies, my friend!"

"Sir Leicester Dedlock, Baronet, how did my calculations come out under these circumstances? When I calculated that this impetuous young woman would overdo it in new directions, was I wrong or right? I was right. What does she try to do? Don't let it give you a turn? To throw the murder on her ladyship."

Sir Leicester rises from his chair and staggers down again.

"And she got encouragement in it from hearing that I was always here, which was done a-purpose. Now, open that pocket-book of mine, Sir Leicester Dedlock, if I may take the liberty of throwing it towards you, and look at the letters sent to me, each with the two words 'Lady Dedlock' in it. Open the one directed to yourself, which I stopped this very morning, and read the three words 'Lady Dedlock, Murderess' in it. These letters have been falling about like a shower of lady-birds. What do you say now to Mrs. Bucket, from her spy-place having seen them all written by this young woman? What do you say to Mrs. Bucket having, within this half-hour, secured the corresponding ink and paper, fellow half-sheets and what not? What do you say to Mrs. Bucket having watched the posting of 'em every one by this young woman, Sir Leicester Dedlock, Baronet?" Mr. Bucket asks triumphant in his admiration of his lady's genius.

Two things are especially observable as Mr. Bucket proceeds to a conclusion. First, that he seems imperceptibly to establish a dreadful right of property in mademoiselle. Secondly, that the very atmosphere she breathes seems to narrow and contract about her as if a close net or a pall were being drawn nearer and yet nearer around her breathless figure.

"There is no doubt that her ladyship was on the spot at the eventful period," says Mr. Bucket, "and my foreign friend here saw her, I believe, from the upper part of the staircase. Her ladyship and George and my foreign friend were all pretty close on one another's heels. But that don't signify any more, so I'll not go into it. I found the wadding of the pistol with which the deceased Mr. Tulkinghorn was shot. It was a bit of the printed description of your house at Chesney Wold. Not much in that, you'll say, Sir Leicester Dedlock, Baronet. No. But when my foreign friend here is so thoroughly off her guard as to think it a safe time to tear up the rest of that leaf, and when Mrs. Bucket puts the pieces together and finds the wadding wanting, it begins to look like Queer Street."

"These are very long lies," mademoiselle interposes. "You prove great deal. Is it that you have almost finished, or are you speaking always?"

"Sir Leicester Dedlock, Baronet," proceeds Mr. Bucket, who delights in a full title and does violence to himself when he dispenses with any fragment of it, "the last point in the case which I am now going to mention shows the necessity of patience in our business, and never doing a thing in a hurry. I watched this young woman yesterday without her knowledge when she was looking at the funeral, in company with my wife, who planned to take her there; and I had so much to convict her, and I saw such an expression in her face, and my mind so rose against her malice towards her ladyship, and the time was altogether such a time for bringing down what you may call retribution upon her, that if I had been a younger hand with less experience, I should have taken her, certain.

"Equally, last night, when her ladyship, as is so universally admired I am sure, come home looking—why, Lord, a man might almost say like Venus rising from the ocean—it was so unpleasant and inconsistent to think of her being charged with a murder of which she was innocent that I felt quite to want to put an end to the job. What should I have lost? Sir Leicester Dedlock, Baronet, I should have lost the weapon. My prisoner here proposed to Mrs. Bucket, after the departure of the funeral, that they should go per bus

a little ways into the country and take tea at a very decent house of
entertainment. Now, near that house of entertainment there's a piece
of water. At tea, my prisoner got up to fetch her pocket handkercher
from the bedroom where the bonnets was; she was rather a long time
gone and came back a little out of wind. As soon as they came home
this was reported to me by Mrs. Bucket, along with her observations
and suspicions. I had the piece of water dragged by moonlight, in
presence of a couple of our men, and the pocket pistol was brought up
before it had been there half-a-dozen hours. Now, my dear, put your
arm a little further through mine, and hold it steady, and I shan't hurt
you!"

In a trice Mr. Bucket snaps a handcuff on her wrist. "That's
one," says Mr. Bucket. "Now the other, darling. Two, and all told!"

He rises; she rises too. "Where," she asks him, darkening her
large eyes until their drooping lids almost conceal them—and yet
they stare, "where is your false, your treacherous, and cursed wife?"

"She's gone forrard to the Police Office," returns Mr. Bucket.
"You'll see her there, my dear."

"I would like to kiss her!" exclaims Mademoiselle Hortense,
panting tigress-like.

"You'd bite her, I suspect," says Mr. Bucket.

"I would!" making her eyes very large. "I would love to tear her
limb from limb."

"Bless you, darling," says Mr. Bucket with the greatest
composure, "I'm fully prepared to hear that. Your sex have such a
surprising animosity against one another when you do differ. You
don't mind me half so much, do you?"

"No. Though you are a devil still."

"Angel and devil by turns, eh?" cries Mr. Bucket. "But I am in
my regular employment, you must consider. Let me put your shawl
tidy. I've been lady's maid to a good many before now. Anything
wanting to the bonnet? There's a cab at the door."

Mademoiselle Hortense, casting an indignant eye at the glass,
shakes herself perfectly neat in one shake and looks, to do her justice,
uncommonly genteel.

"Listen then, my angel," says she after several sarcastic nods.
"You are very spiritual. But can you restore him back to life?"

Mr. Bucket answers, "Not exactly."

"That is droll. Listen yet one time. You are very spiritual. Can you make an honourable lady of her?"

"Don't be malicious," says Mr. Bucket.

"Or a haughty gentlemen of *him*?" cries mademoiselle, referring to Sir Leicester with ineffable disdain. "Eh! Oh, then regard him! The poor infant! Ha! Ha! Ha!"

"Come, come, why this is worse *parlaying* than the other," says Mr. Bucket. "Come along!"

"You cannot do these things? Then you can do as you please with me. It is but the death, it is all the same. Let us go, my angel. Adieu, you old man, grey. I pity you, and I despise you!"

With these last words she snaps her teeth together as if her mouth closed with a spring. It is impossible to describe how Mr. Bucket gets her out, but he accomplishes that feat in a manner so peculiar to himself, enfolding and pervading her like a cloud, and hovering away with her as if he were a homely Jupiter and she the object of his affections.

Sir Leicester, left alone, remains in the same attitude, as though he were still listening and his attention were still occupied. At length he gazes round the empty room, and finding it deserted, rises unsteadily to his feet, pushes back his chair, and walks a few steps, supporting himself by the table. Then he stops, and with more of those inarticulate sounds, lifts up his eyes and seems to stare at something.

He sees her, almost to the exclusion of himself, and cannot bear to look upon her cast down from the high place she has graced so well.

And even to the point of his sinking on the ground, oblivious to his suffering, he can yet pronounce her name with something like distinctness in the midst of those intrusive sounds, and in a tone of mourning and compassion rather than reproach.

The Stolen Letter

WILKIE COLLINS

Although (William) Wilkie Collins (1824–1889) will always be best known for the creation of Sergeant Cuff in *The Moonstone* (1868), he followed Edgar Allan Poe's lead twelve years earlier in writing a detective short story in a similar vein, producing a counterpoint to "The Purloined Letter" in "The Stolen Letter" (1865), which likewise involves a blackmail letter to be retrieved by the detective. Collins builds the story in exactly the opposite manner to Poe. In Collins, the deduction must be applied to the step-by-step search for an out-of-sight document. The result is an extremely modern story line with only slight apologies to Edgar Allan Poe, who supplied the title and the central theme.

As for Collins's masterpiece, *The Moonstone*, it is the closest thing to a detective novel produced prior to the appearance of Sherlock Holmes in *A Study in Scarlet* (1887). Technically, since it contains a great deal of material extraneous to the solution of the mystery, it cannot be called a detective novel per se, in the purist tradition. It should be read in its entirety as an example of the almost-detective-genre years before its time. Collins's other noteworthy work, *The Woman in White* (1860), is a supremely satisfying suspense novel involving an imprisoned heroine and a sinister European count; it too should be read in its entirety.

I served my time, never mind in whose office, and started in business for myself in one of our English country towns, I decline stating which. I hadn't a farthing of capital, and my friends in the neighborhood were poor and useless enough, with one exception. That exception was Mr. Frank Gatliffe, son of Mr. Gatliffe, member for the county, the richest man and the proudest for many a mile round and about our parts. Stop a bit, Mr. Artist, you needn't perk up and look knowing. You won't trace any particulars by the name of Gatliffe. I'm not bound to commit myself or anybody else by mentioning names. I have given you the first that came into my head.

Well, Mr. Frank was a staunch friend of mine, and ready to recommend me whenever he got the chance. I had contrived to get him a little timely help, for a consideration, of course, in borrowing at a fair rate of interest; in fact, I had saved him from the moneylenders. The money was borrowed while Mr. Frank was at college. He came back from college, and stopped at home a little while and then there got spread about all our neighborhood a report that he had fallen in love, as the saying is, with his young sister's governess, and that his mind was made up to marry her. What! you're at it again, Mr. Artist! You want to know her name, don't you? What do you think of Smith?

Speaking as a lawyer, I consider report, in a general way, to be a fool and a liar. But in this case report turned out to be something very different. Mr. Frank told me he was really in love, and said upon his honor (an absurd expression which young chaps of his age are always using) he was determined to marry Smith, the governess, the sweet darling girl, as he called her; but I'm not sentimental, and I call her Smith, the governess. Well, Mr. Frank's father, being as proud as Lucifer, said "No," as to marrying the governess, when Mr. Frank wanted him to say "Yes." He was a man of business, was old Gatliffe, and he took the proper business course. He sent the governess away with a first-rate character and a spanking present, and then he looked about him to get something for Mr. Frank to do. While he was looking about, Mr. Frank bolted to London after the governess, who had nobody belonging to her to go to but an aunt, her father's sister. The aunt refuses to let Mr. Frank in without the squire's permission. Mr. Frank writes to his father, and says he will marry the girl as soon as he is of age, or shoot himself. Up to town comes the squire and his wife and his daughter, and a lot of sentimentality, not in the slightest degree material to the present statement, takes places among them, and the upshot of it is that old Gatliffe is forced into withdrawing the word No, and substituting the word Yes.

I don't believe he would ever have done it, though, but for one lucky peculiarity in the case. The governess's father was a man of good family, pretty nigh as good as Gatliffe's own. He had been in the army, had sold out; set up as a wine-merchant, failed, died; ditto his wife, as to the dying part of it. No relation, in fact, left for the squire to make inquiries about but the father's sister, who had behaved, as old Gatliffe said, like a thorough-bred gentlewoman in shutting the door against Mr. Frank in the first instance. So, to cut the matter short, things were at last made up pleasant enough. The time was fixed for the wedding, and an announcement about it, Marriage in High Life and all that, put into the county paper. There was a regular biography, besides, of the governess's father, so as to stop people from talking, a great flourish about his pedigree, and a long account of his services in the army; but not a word, mind ye, of his having turned wine-merchant afterward. Oh, no, not a word about that!

I knew it, though, for Mr. Frank told me. He hadn't a bit of pride about him. He introduced me to his future wife one day when I met him out walking, and asked me if I did not think he was a lucky fellow. I don't mind admitting that I did, and I told him so. Ah! but she was one of my sort, was that governess. Stood, to the best of my recollection, five foot four. Good lissom figure, that looked as if it had never been boxed up in a pair of stays. Eyes that made me feel as if I was under a pretty stiff cross examination the moment she looked at me. Fine, red, kiss-and-come-again sort of lips. Cheeks and complexion, no, Mr. Artist, you wouldn't identify her by her cheeks and complexion, if I drew you a picture of them this very moment. She has had a family of children since the time I'm talking of; and her cheeks are a trifle fatter; and her complexion is a shade or two redder now, than when I first met her out walking with Mr. Frank.

The marriage was to take place on a Wednesday. I decline mentioning the year or the month. I had started as an attorney on my own account, say six weeks, more or less, and was sitting alone in my office on the Monday morning before the wedding day, trying to see my way clear before me and not succeeding particularly well, when Mr. Frank suddenly bursts in, as white as any ghost that ever was painted, and says he's got the most dreadful case for me to advise on, and not an hour to lose in acting on my advice.

"Is this in the way of business, Mr. Frank?" says I, stopping him just as he was beginning to get sentimental. "Yes or no, Mr. Frank?"

rapping my new office paper-knife on the table, to pull him up short all the sooner.

"My dear fellow," he was always familiar with me, "it's in the way of business, certainly; but friendship...."

I was obliged to pull him up short again, and regularly examine him as if he had been in the witness-box, or he would have kept me talking to no purpose half the day.

"Now, Mr. Frank," says I, "I can't have any sentimentality mixed up with business matters. You please stop talking, and let me ask questions. Answer in the fewest words you can use. Nod when nodding will do instead of words."

I fixed him with my eye for about three seconds, as he sat groaning and wriggling in his chair. When I'd done fixing him, I gave another rap with my paper-knife on the table to startle him a bit. Then I went on.

"From what you have been stating up to the present time," says I, "I gather that you are in a scrape which is likely to interfere seriously with your marriage on Wednesday?"

(He nodded, and I cut in again before he could say a word):

"The scrape affects your young lady, and goes back to the period of a transaction in which her late father was engaged, doesn't it?"

(He nods, and I cut in once more):

"There is a party, who turned up after seeing the announcement of your marriage in the paper, who is cognizant of what he oughtn't to know, and who is prepared to use his knowledge of the same to the prejudice of the young lady and of your marriage, unless he receives a sum of money to quiet him? Very well. Now, first of all, Mr. Frank, state what you have been told by the young lady herself about the transaction of her late father. How did you first come to have any knowledge of it?"

"She was talking to me about her father one day so tenderly and prettily, that she quite excited my interest about him," begins Mr. Frank; "and I asked her, among other things, what had occasioned his death. She said she believed it was distress of mind in the first instance; and added that this distress was connected with a shocking secret, which she and her mother had kept from everybody, but which she could not keep from me, because she was determined to begin her married life by having no secrets from her husband." Here

Mr. Frank began to get sentimental again, and I pulled him up short once more with the paper-knife.

"She told me," Mr. Frank went on, "that the great mistake of her father's life was his selling out of the army and taking to the wine trade. He had no talent for the business; things went wrong with him from the first. His clerk, it was strongly suspected, cheated him...."

"Stop a bit," says I. "What was that suspected clerk's name?"

"Davager," says he.

"Davager," says I, making a note of it. "Go on, Mr. Frank."

"His affairs got more and more entangled," says Mr. Frank; "he was pressed for money in all directions; bankruptcy, and consequent dishonor (as he considered it) stared him in the face. His mind was so affected by his troubles that both his wife and daughter, toward the last, considered him to be hardly responsible for his own acts. In this state of desperation and misery, he...." Here Mr. Frank began to hesitate.

We have two ways in the law of drawing evidence off nice and clear from an unwilling client or witness. We give him a fright, or we treat him to a joke. I treated Mr. Frank to a joke.

"Ah!" says I, "I know what he did. He had a signature to write; and by the most natural mistake in the world, he wrote another gentleman's name instead of his own, eh?"

"It was to a bill," says Mr. Frank, looking very crestfallen, instead of taking the joke. "His principal creditor wouldn't wait till he could raise the money, or the greater part of it. But he was resolved, if he sold off everything, to get the amount and repay...."

"Of course," says I, "drop that. The forgery was discovered. When?"

"Before even the first attempt was made to negotiate the bill. He had done the whole thing in the most absurdly and innocently wrong way. The person whose name he had used was a staunch friend of his, and a relation of his wife's, a good man as well as a rich one. He had influence with the chief creditor, and he used it nobly. He had a real affection for the unfortunate man's wife, and he proved it generously."

"Come to the point," says I. "What did he do? In a business way, what did he do?"

"He put the false bill into the fire, drew a bill of his own to replace it, and then, only then, told my dear girl and her mother all that had happened. Can you imagine anything nobler?" asks Mr. Frank.

"Speaking in my professional capacity, I can't imagine anything greener!" says I. "Where was the father? Off, I suppose?"

"Ill in bed," says Mr. Frank, coloring. "But he mustered strength enough to write a contrite and grateful letter the same day, promising to prove himself worthy of the noble moderation and forgiveness extended to him, by selling off everything he possessed to repay his money debt. He did sell off everything, down to some old family pictures that were heirlooms; down to the little plate he had; down to the very tables and chairs that furnished his drawing room. Every farthing of the debt was paid; and he was left to begin the world again, with the kindest promises of help from the generous man who had forgiven him. It was too late. His crime of one rash moment, atoned for though it had been, preyed upon his mind. He became possessed with the idea that he had lowered himself forever in the estimation of his wife and daughter, and...."

"He died," I cut in. "Yes, yes, we know that. Let's go back for a minute to the contrite and grateful letter that he wrote. My experience in the law, Mr. Frank, has convinced me that if everybody burned everybody else's letters, half the courts of justice in this country might shut up shop. Do you happen to know whether the letter we are now speaking of contained anything like an avowal or confession of the forgery?"

"Of course it did," says he. "Could the writer express his contrition properly without making some such confession?"

"Quite easy, if he had been a lawyer," says I. "But never mind that; I'm going to make a guess, a desperate guess, mind. Should I be altogether in error if I thought that this letter had been stolen; and that the fingers of Mr. Davager, of suspicious commercial celebrity, might possibly be the fingers which took it?"

"That is exactly what I wanted to make you understand," cried Mr. Frank.

"How did he communicate the interesting fact of the theft to you?"

"He has not ventured into my presence. The scoundrel actually had the audacity...."

"Aha!" says I. "The young lady herself! Sharp practitioner, Mr. Davager."

"Early this morning, when she was walking alone in the shrubbery," Mr. Frank goes on, "he had the assurance to approach her, and to say that he had been watching his opportunity of getting a private interview for days past. He then showed her, actually showed her, her unfortunate father's letter; put into her hand another letter directed to me; bowed and walked off; leaving her half dead with astonishment and terror. If I had only happened to be there at the time!" says Mr. Frank, shaking his fist murderously in the air, by way of a finish.

"It's the greatest luck in the world that you were not," says I. "Have you got that other letter?"

He handed it to me. It was so remarkably humorous and short, that I remember every word of it at this distance of time. It began in this way:

"To Francis Gatliffe, Esq., Jun.

"Sir, I have an extremely curious and autograph letter to sell. The price is five-hundred-pound note. The young lady to whom you are to be married on Wednesday will inform you of the nature of the letter, and the genuineness of the autograph. If you refuse to deal, I shall send a copy to the local paper, and shall wait on your highly-respected father with the original curiosity, on the afternoon of Tuesday next. Having come down here on family business, I have put up at the family hotel, being to be heard of at the Gatliffe Arms.

Your very obedient servant,
Alfred Davager."

"A clever fellow that," says I, putting the letter in my private drawer.

"Clever!" cried Mr. Frank, "he ought to be horsewhipped within an inch of his life. I would have done it myself; but she made me promise, before she told me a word of the matter, to come straight to you."

"That was one of the wisest promises you ever made," says I. "We can't afford to bully this fellow, whatever else we may do with him. Do you think I am saying anything libelous against your excellent father's character when I assert that if he saw the letter he would certainly insist on your marriage being put off, at the very least."

"Feeling as my father does about my marriage, he would insist on its being dropped altogether, if he saw this letter," says Mr. Frank, with a groan. "But even that is not the worst of it. The generous, noble girl says that if the letter appears in the paper, with all the unanswerable comments this scoundrel would be sure to add to it, she would rather die than hold me to my engagement, even if my father would let me keep it."

As he said this his eyes began to water. He was a weak young fellow, and ridiculously fond of her. I brought him back to business with another rap of the paper-knife.

"Hold up, Mr. Frank," says I. "I have a question or two more. Did you think of asking the young lady whether, to the best of her knowledge, this infernal letter was the only written evidence of the forgery now in existence?"

"Yes, I did think directly of asking her that," says he; "and she told me she was quite certain that there was no written evidence of the forgery except that one letter."

"Will you give Mr. Davager his price for it?" says I.

"Yes," says Mr. Frank, quite peevish with me for asking him such a question. He was an easy young chap in money matters, and talked of hundreds as most men talk of sixpence.

"Mr. Frank," says I, "you came here to get my help and advice in this extremely ticklish business, and you are ready, as I know without asking, to remunerate me for all and any of my services at the usual professional rate. Now, I've made up my mind to act boldly, desperately, if you like, on the hit or miss, win all or lose all principle, in dealing with this matter. Here is my proposal. I'm going to try if I can't do Mr. Davager out of his letter. If I don't succeed before tomorrow afternoon, you hand him the money, and I charge you nothing for professional services. If I do succeed, I hand you the letter instead of Mr. Davager, and you give me the money instead of giving it to him. It's a precious risk for me, but I am ready to run it. You must pay your five hundred any way. What do you say to my plan? Is it Yes, Mr. Frank, or No?"

"Hang your questions!" cries Mr. Frank, jumping up: "you know it's Yes ten thousand times over. Only you earn the money and...."

"And you will be too glad to give it to me. Very good. Now go home. Comfort the young lady, don't let Mr. Davager so much as set eyes on you, keep quiet, leave everything to me. And feel as certain as you please that all the letters in the world can't stop your being married on Wednesday." With these words I hustled him off out of the office, for I wanted to be left alone to make my mind up about what I should do.

The first thing, of course, was to have a look at the enemy. I wrote to Mr. Davager, telling him that I was privately appointed to arrange the little business matter between himself and "another party" (no names!) on friendly terms; and begging him to call on me at his earliest convenience. At the very beginning of the case, Mr. Davager bothered me. His answer was, that it would not be convenient for him to call till between six and seven in the evening. In this way, you see, he contrived to make me lose several precious hours, at a time when minutes almost were of importance. I had nothing for it but to be patient, and to give certain instructions, before Mr. Davager came, to my boy Tom.

There never was such a sharp boy of fourteen before, and there never will be again, as my boy Tom. A spy to look after Mr. Davager was, of course, the first requisite in a case of this kind; and Tom was the smallest, quickest, quietest, sharpest, stealthiest little snake of a chap that ever dogged a gentleman's steps, and kept cleverly out of range of a gentleman's eyes. I settled it with the boy that he was not to show up at all when Mr. Davager came; and that he was to wait to hear me ring the bell when Mr. Davager left. If I rang twice, he was to show the gentleman out. If I rang once, he was to keep out of the way, and follow the gentleman wherever he went till he got back to the inn. Those were the only preparations I could make to begin with; being obliged to wait, and let myself be guided by what turned up.

About a quarter to seven my gentleman came.

In the profession of the law we get somehow quite remarkably mixed up with ugly people, blackguard people, and dirty people. But far away the ugliest and dirtiest blackguard I ever saw in my life was Mr. Alfred Davager. He had greasy white hair and a mottled face. He was low in the forehead, fat in the stomach, hoarse in the voice, and weak in the legs. Both his eyes were bloodshot, and one was fixed in his head. He smelled of spirits, and carried a tooth-pick in his mouth. "How are you? I've just done dinner," says he; and he lights a cigar, sits down with his legs crossed, and winks at me.

I tried at first to take the measure of him in a wheedling, confidential way; but it was no good. I asked him, in a facetious, smiling manner, how he had got hold of the letter. He only told me in answer that he had been in the confidential employment of the writer of it, and that he had always been famous since infancy for a sharp eye to his own interests. I paid him some compliments; but he was not to be flattered. I tried to make him lose his temper; but he kept it in spite of me. It ended in his driving me to my last resource: I made an attempt to frighten him.

"Before we say a word about the money," I began, "let me put a case, Mr. Davager. The pull you have on Mr. Francis Gatliffe is, that you can hinder his marriage on Wednesday. Now, suppose I have got a magistrate's warrant to apprehend you in my pocket? Suppose I have a constable to execute it in the next room? Suppose I bring you up tomorrow, the day before the marriage, charge you only generally with an attempt to extort money, and apply for a day's remand to complete the case? Suppose, as a suspicious stranger, you can't get bail in this town? Suppose...."

"Stop a bit," says Mr. Davager. "Suppose I should not be the greenest fool that ever stood in shoes? Suppose I should not carry the letter about me? Suppose I should have given a certain envelope to a certain friend of mind in a certain place in this town? Suppose the letter should be inside that envelope, directed to old Gatliffe, side by side with a copy of the letter directed to the editor of the local paper? Suppose my friend should be instructed to open the envelope, and take the letters to their right address, if I don't appear to claim them from him this evening? In short, my dear sir, suppose you were born yesterday, and suppose I wasn't?" says Mr. Davager, and winks at me again.

He didn't take me by surprise, for I never expected that he had the letter about him. I made a pretense of being very much taken aback, and of being quite ready to give in. We settled our business about delivering the letter, and handing over the money, in no time. I was to draw out a document, which he was to sign. He knew the document was stuff and nonsense, just as well as I did, and told me I was only proposing it to swell my client's bill. Sharp as he was, he was wrong there. The document was not to be drawn out to gain money from Mr. Frank, but to gain time from Mr. Davager. It served me as an excuse to put off the payment of the five hundred pounds till three o'clock on the Tuesday afternoon. The Tuesday morning Mr.

Davager said he should devote to his amusement, and asked me what sights were to be seen in the neighborhood of the town. When I had told him, he pitched his toothpick into my grate, yawned, and went out.

I rang the bell once, waited till he had passed the window, and then looked after Tom. There was my jewel of a boy on the opposite side of the street, just getting his top going in the most playful manner possible. Mr. Davager walked away up the street toward the market-place. Tom whipped his top up the street toward the market-place too.

In a quarter of an hour he came back, with all his evidence collected in a beautifully clear and compact manner. Mr. Davager had walked to the public-house just outside the town, in a lane leading to the high-road. On a bench outside the public house there sat a man smoking. He says "All right?" and gave a letter to Mr. Davager, who answered "All right!" and walked back to the inn. In the hall he ordered hot rum-and-water, cigars, slippers, and a fire to be lit in his room. After that he went upstairs, and Tom came away.

I now saw my road before me, not very far on, but still clear. I had housed the letter, in all probability for that night, at the Gatliffe Arms. After tipping Tom, I gave him directions to play about the door of the inn, and refresh himself when he was tired at the tart-shop opposite, eating as much as he pleased, on the understanding that he crammed all the time with his eyes on the window. If Mr. Davager went out, or Mr. Davager's friend called on him, Tom was to let me know. He was also to take a little note from me to the head chambermaid, an old friend of mine, asking her to step over to my office, on a private matter of business, as soon as her work was done for that night. After settling these little matters, having an hour to spare, I turned to and did myself a bloater at the office fire, and had a drop of gin-and-water hot, and felt comparatively happy.

When the head chambermaid came, it turned out, as good, as good luck would have it, that Mr. Davager had drawn her attention rather too closely to his ugliness, by offering her a testimony of his regard in the shape of a kiss. I no sooner mentioned him than she flew into a passion; and when I added, by way of clinching the matter, that I was retained to defend the interests of a very beautiful and deserving young lady (name not referred to, of course) against the most cruel underhand treachery on the part of Mr. Davager, the head chamber-

maid was ready to go any lengths that she could safely to serve my
cause. In a few words I discovered that Boots was to call Mr. Davager
at eight the next morning, and was to take his clothes downstairs to
brush as usual. If Mr. D. had not emptied his own pockets overnight,
we arranged that Boots was to forget to employ them for him, and
was to bring the clothes downstairs just as he found them. If Mr. D.'s
pockets were emptied, then, of course, it would be necessary to
transfer the searching process to Mr. D.'s room. Under any circumstances, I was certain of the head chambermaid; and under any
circumstances, also, the head chambermaid was certain of Boots.

I waited till Tom came home, looking very puffy and bilious
about the face; but as to his intellects, if anything, rather sharper than
ever. His report was uncommonly short and pleasant. The inn was
shutting up; Mr. Davager was going to bed in rather a drunken
condition; Mr. Davager's friend had never appeared. I sent Tom
(properly instructed about keeping our man in view all the next
morning) to his shake-down behind the office-desk, where I heard
him hiccoughing half the night, as even the best boys will, when
over-excited and too full of tarts.

At half-past seven next morning, I slipped quietly into Boots's
pantry.

Down came the clothes. No pockets in trousers. Waistcoat-
pockets empty. Coat-pockets with something in them. First, handkerchief; secondly, bunch of keys; thirdly, cigar-case; fourthly,
pocketbook. Of course I wasn't such a fool as to expect to find the
letter there, but I opened the pocketbook with a certain curiosity,
notwithstanding.

Nothing in the two pockets of the book but some old
advertisements cut out of newspapers, a lock of hair tied round with a
dirty bit of ribbon, a circular letter about a loan society, and some
copies of verses not likely to suit any company that was not of an
extremely free-and-easy description. On the leaves of the pocket-
book, people's addresses scrawled in pencil, and bets jotted down in
red ink. On one leaf, by itself, this queer inscription:

"Mem. 5 Along. 4 Across."

I understood everything, but those words and figures, so of
course I copied them out into my own book.

Then I waited in the pantry till Boots had brushed the clothes, and had taken them upstairs. His report when he came down was, that Mr. D. had asked if it was a fine morning. Being told that it was, he had ordered breakfast at nine, and a saddle horse to be at the door at ten, to take him to Grimwith Abbey, one of the sights in the neighborhood which I had told him of the evening before.

"I'll be here, coming in by the back way, at half-past ten," says I to the head chambermaid.

"What for?" says she.

"To take the responsibility of making Mr. Davager's bed off your hands for this morning only," said I.

"Any more orders?" says she.

"One more," says I. "I want to hire Sam for the morning. Put it down in the order-book that he's to be brought round to my office at ten."

In case you would think Sam was a man, I'd better perhaps tell you he was a pony. I'd made up my mind that it would be beneficial to Tom's health, after the tarts, if he took a constitutional airing on a nice hard saddle in the direction of Grimwith Abbey.

"Anything else?" says the head chambermaid.

"Only one more favor," says I, "would my Tom be very much in the way if he came, from now till ten, to help with the boots and shoes, and stood at his work close by this window which looks out on the staircase?"

"Not a bit," says the head chambermaid.

"Thank you," says I; and stepped back to my office directly. When I had sent Tom off to help with the boots and shoes, I reviewed the whole case exactly as it stood at that time.

There were three things Mr. Davager might do with the letter. He might give it to his friend again before ten, in which case Tom would most likely see the said friend on the stairs. He might take it to his friend, or to some other friend, after ten, in which case Tom was ready to follow him on Sam the pony. And, lastly, he might leave it hidden somewhere in the room at the inn, in which case I was all ready for him with a search-warrant of my own granting under favor always of my friend the head chambermaid. So far I had my business arrangements all gathered up nice and compact in my own hands. Only two things bothered me; the terrible shortness of the time at my disposal, in case I failed in my first experiments, for getting hold of the letter, and that queer inscription which I had copied out of the pocket book: "Mem. 5 Along. 4 Across."

It was the measuring most likely of something, and he was afraid of forgetting it; therefore it was something important. Query, something about himself? Say "5" (inches) "along," he doesn't wear a wig. Say "5" (feet) "along," it can't be a coat, waistcoat, trousers, or underclothing. Say "5" (yards) "along," it can't be anything about himself, unless he wears round his body the rope that he's sure to be hanged with one of these days. Then it is not something about himself. What do I know of what is important to him besides? I know of nothing but the Letter. Can the memorandum be connected with that? Say, yes. What do "5" along and "4" across mean, then? The measurement of something he carries about with him? or the measurement of something in his room? I could get pretty satis- factorily to myself as far as that; but I could get no further.

Tom came back to the office, and reported him mounted for his ride. His friend had never appeared. I sent the boy off, with his proper instructions, on Sam's back, wrote an encouraging letter to Mr. Frank to keep him quiet, then slipped into the inn by the back way a little before half-past ten. The head chambermaid gave me a signal when the landing was clear. I got into his room without a soul but her seeing me, and locked the door immediately.

The case was, to a certain extent, simplified now. Either Mr. Davager had ridden out with the letter about him, or he had left it in some safe hiding-place in his room. I suspected it to be in his room for a reason that will a little astonish you: his trunk, his dressing-case, and all the drawers and cupboards, were left open. I knew my customer, and I thought this extraordinary carelessness on his part rather suspicious.

Mr. Davager had taken one of the best bedrooms at the Gatliffe Arms. Floor carpeted all over, walls beautifully papered, four-poster bed, and general furniture first-rate. I searched, to begin with, on the usual plan, examining everything in every possible way, and taking more than an hour about it. No discovery. Then I pulled out a carpenter's rule which I had brought with me. Was there anything in the room which, either in inches, feet, or yards, answered to "5 along" and "4 across"? Nothing. I put the rule back in my pocket, measurement was no good, evidently. Was there anything in the room that would count up to 5 one way and 4 another, seeing that nothing would measure up to it? I had got obstinately persuaded by this time that the letter must be in the room, principally because of the trouble I had had in looking for it. And persuaded myself of that, I took it into my head next, just as obstinately, that "5 along" and "4 across" must be the right clew to find the letter by, principally because I hadn't left myself, after my searching and thinking, even so much as the ghost of another guide to go by. "Five along"; where could I count five along the room, in any part of it?

Not on the papers. The pattern there was pillars of trellis-work and flowers, inclosing a plain green ground, only four pillars along the wall and only two across. The furniture? There were not five chairs or five separate pieces of any furniture in the room altogether. The fringes that hung from the cornice of the bed? Plenty of them, at any rate! Up I jumped on the counterpane, with my pen-knife in my hand. Every way that "5 along" and "4 across" could be reckoned on those unlucky fringes I reckoned on them, probed with my knife, scratched with my penknife, scratched with my nails, crunched with my fingers. No use; not a sign of a letter; and the time was getting on, oh, Lord! how the time did get on in Mr. Davager's room that morning.

I jumped down from the bed, so desperate at my ill luck that I hardly cared whether anybody heard me or not. Quite a little cloud of dust rose at my feet as they thumped on the carpet.

"Hullo!" thought I, "my friend the head chambermaid takes it easy here. Nice state for a carpet to be in, in one of the best bedrooms at the Gatliffe Arms." Carpet! I had been jumping up on the bed, and staring up at the walls, but I had never so much as given a glance down at the carpet. Think of me pretending to be a lawyer, and not knowing how to look low enough!

The carpet! It had been a stout article in its time; had evidently begun in a drawing-room; then descended to a coffee-room; then gone upstairs altogether to a bedroom. The ground was brown, and the pattern was bunches of leaves and roses speckled over the ground at regular distances. I reckoned up the bunches. Ten along the room, eight across it. When I had stepped out five one way and four the other, and was down on my knees on the center bunch, as true as I sit on this chair I could hear my own heart beating so loud that it quite frightened me.

I looked narrowly all over the bunch, and I felt all over it with the ends of my fingers, and nothing came out of it. Then I scraped it over slowly and gently with my nails. My second finger-nail stuck a little at one place. I parted the pile of the carpet over that place, and saw a thin slit which had been hidden by the pile being smoothed over it, a slit about half an inch long, with a little end of brown thread, exactly the color of the carpet ground, sticking out about a quarter of an inch from the middle of it. Just as I laid hold of the thread gently, I heard a footstep outside the door.

It was only the head chambermaid. "Haven't you done yet?" she whispers.

"Give me two minutes," says I, "and don't let anybody come near the door, whatever you do, don't let anybody startle me again by coming near the door."

I took a little pull at the thread, and heard something rustle. I took a longer pull, and out came a piece of paper, rolled up tight like those candle-lighters that the ladies make. I unrolled it; and, by George! there was the letter!

The original letter! I knew it by the color of the ink. The letter that was worth five hundred pounds to me! It was all that I could do to keep myself at first from throwing my hat into the air, and hurrahing like mad. I had to take a chair and sit quiet in it for a minute or two, before I could cool myself down again when I found myself pondering how to let Mr. Davager know that he had been done by the innocent country attorney, after all.

It was not long before a nice irritating plan occurred to me. I tore a blank leaf out of my pocket book, and wrote on it with my pencil, "Change for a five-hundred-pound note," folded up the paper, tied the thread to it, poked it back into the hiding-place, smoothed over the pile of the carpet, and then bolted off to Mr. Frank. He in his turn bolted off to show the letter to the young lady, who first certified to its genuineness, then dropped it into the fire, and then took the initiative for the first time since her marriage engagement, by flinging her arms round his neck, kissing him with all her might, and going into hysterics in his arms. So at least Mr. Frank told me, but that's not evidence. It is evidence, however, that I saw them married with my own eyes on the Wednesday; and that while they went off in a carriage-and-four to spend the honeymoon, I went off on my own legs to open a credit at the Town and County Bank with a five-and-hundred pound note in my pocket.

As to Mr. Davager, I can tell you nothing more about him,

except what is derived from hearsay evidence, which is always unsatisfactory evidence, even in a lawyer's mouth.

My inestimable boy, Tom, although twice kicked off by Sam the pony, never lost hold of the bridle, and kept his man in sight from first to last. He had nothing particular to report except that on the way out to the Abbey Mr. Davager had stopped at the public-house, had spoken a word or two to his friend of the night before, and had handed him what looked like a bit of paper. This was no doubt a clew to the thread that held the letter, to be used in case of accidents. In every other respect Mr. D. had ridden out and ridden in like an ordinary sightseer. Tom reported him to me as having dismounted at the hotel about two. At half-past I locked my office door, nailed a card under the knocker with "not at home till tomorrow" written on it, and retired to a friend's house a mile or so out of town for the rest of the day.

Mr. Davager, I have been since given to understand, left the Gatliffe Arms, that same night, with his best clothes on his back, and with all the valuable contents of his dressing-case in his pockets. I am not in a condition to state whether he ever went through the form of asking for his bill or not; but I can positively testify that he never paid it; and that the effects left in his bedroom did not pay it either. When I add to these fragments of evidence that he and I have never met (luckily for me, you will say) since I jockeyed him out of his bank-note, I have about fulfilled my implied contract as maker of a statement. Observe the expression, will you? I said it was a Statement before I began; and I say, it's a Statement now I've done. I defy you to prove it's a Story! How are you getting on with my portrait? I like you very well, Mr. Artist; but if you have been taking advantage of my talking to shirk your work, as sure as you're alive I'll split upon you to the Town Council!

I attended a great many times at my queer sitter's house before his likeness was completed. To the last he was dissatisfied with the progress I made. Fortunately for me, the Town Council approved of the portrait when it was done. Mr. Boxsious, however, objected to them as being much too easy to please. He did not dispute the fidelity of the likeness, but he asserted that I had not covered the canvas with half paint enough for my money. To this day (for he is still alive), he describes me to all inquiring friends as "The Painter-Man who jockeyed the Town Council."

The Unmasking of Thorn

From *East Lynne*

MRS. HENRY WOOD

Mrs. Henry Wood (1814–1887) was born Ellen Price, and as Mrs. Henry Wood wrote some thirty-five popular novels during her lifetime. Working in the flowery Victorian tradition, she created novels for women readers portraying conventional romances that were then called "sensational" novels ("sensation" in the sense of "feeling"), and would now be called "soap opera" serials. As a novel and as a play, *East Lynne* (1861) became staple fare for many years, and stands as the epitome of the nineteenth-century tearjerker— featuring the fallen wife/adulterer, the accused innocent, the child out of wedlock.

The novel's main plot concerns a fallen woman returned incognito to care for her children; but woven through it is a solid detective plot involving an innocent man accused of murder. The actual murderer is Francis Levison; the accused man, Richard Hare, knows him simply as "Thorn." In this excerpt Lawyer Ball employs deduction during a courtroom interrogation to extract the truth from a pair of reluctant witnesses.

The magistrates took their seats on the bench. The bench would not hold them; all in the Commission of the Peace flocked in. As to the

161

room, the wonder was how it ever got emptied again, so densely was it packed. Sir Francis Levison's friends were there in a body. They did not believe a word of the accusation. Lord Mount Severn, who chose to be present, had a place assigned him on the bench. Lord Vane got the best place he could fight for amidst the crowd. Mr. Justice Hare [father of the accused Richard] sat as chairman, usually stern, unbending and grim. No favor would he show, but no unfairness. Had it been to save his son from hanging he would not adjudge guilt to Francis Levison against his conscience. Colonel Bethel was likewise on the bench, stern also. Mr. Rubiny watched the case on behalf of Sir Francis Levison.

Mr. Ball opened the proceedings, giving the account which had been imparted to him by Richard Hare, but not mentioning Richard as his informant. He was questioned as to whence he obtained his information, but replied that it was not convenient at present to disclose the source. The stumbling block to the magistrates appeared to be the identifying Levison with Thorn. Ebenezer James came forward to prove it.

"What do you know of the prisoner, Sir Francis Levison?" questioned Justice Herbert.

"Not much," responded Mr. Ebenezer. "I used to know him as Captain Thorn."

"Captain Thorn?"

"Afy Hallijohn called him captain, but I understood he was but a lieutenant."

"From whom did you understand that?"

"From Afy. She was the only person I heard speak of him."

"And you say you were in the habit of seeing him in the place mentioned, the Abbey Wood?"

"I saw him there repeatedly; also at Hallijohn's cottage."

"Did you speak with him as Thorn?"

"Two or three times. I addressed him as Thorn, and he answered to the name. I had no suspicion but what it was his name. Otway Bethel"—casting his eyes on Mr. Otway, who stood in his shaggy attire—"also knew him as Thorn. And so, I make no doubt, did Locksley, for he was always in the wood."

"Anybody else?"

"Poor Hallijohn himself knew him as Thorn. He said to Afy one day in my presence that he would not have that confounded dandy, Thorn, coming there."

"Were those the words he used?"

"They were. 'That confounded dandy, Thorn!' I remember Afy's reply. It was rather insolent. She said Thorn was as free to come there as anybody else. And she would not be found fault with as though she was not fit to take care of herself."

"That is nothing to the purpose. Were any others acquainted with this Thorn?"

"I should imagine the elder sister, Joyce, was. And the one who knew him best of all was young Richard Hare."

Old Richard Hare from his place on the bench frowned menacingly at an imaginary Richard.

"What took Thorn into the woods so often?"

"He was courting Afy."

"With an intention of marrying her?"

"Well—no," cried Mr. Ebenezer, with a twist of the mouth. "I should not suppose he entertained any intention of that sort. He used to come over from Swainson, or its neighborhood, riding a splendid horse."

"Whom did you suppose him to be?"

"I supposed him to be moving in the upper ranks of life. There was no doubt of it. His dress, his manners, his tone, all proclaimed it. He appeared to wish to shun observation, and evidently did not care to be seen. He rarely arrived until twilight."

"Did you see him there on the night of Hallijohn's murder?"

"No, I was not there myself that evening, so could not have seen him."

"Did a suspicion cross your mind at any time that he may have been guilty of the murder?"

"Never. Richard Hare was accused of it, and it never occurred to me to suppose that he had not done it."

"Pray, how many years is this ago?" sharply interrupted Mr. Rubiny, perceiving that the witness was done with.

"Let's see!" responded Mr. Ebenezer. "I can't be sure as to a year without reckoning up. A dozen, if not more."

"And you mean to say that you can swear to Sir Francis Levison being that man—with all those years intervening?"

"I swear that he is the same man. I am as positive of his identity as I am of my own."

"Without having seen him from that time to this?" derisively returned the lawyer. "Nonsense, witness!"

"I did not say that," returned Mr. Ebenezer.

The court pricked up its ears.

"Have you seen him between then and now?" asked one of them.

"Once."

"Where and when?"

"It was in London. About eighteen months after the period of the murder."

"What communication had you with him?"

"None at all. I only saw him. Quite by chance."

"And whom did you suppose him to be—Thorn—or Levison?"

"Thorn, certainly. I never dreamed of his being Levison until he appeared here now to oppose Carlyle [in the current election]."

A wild, savage curse shot through Sir Francis' heart as he heard the words. What demon had possessed him to venture his neck into the lion's den? There had been a strong, hidden power holding him back from it independent of his dislike to face Mr. Carlyle. How could he have been so mad as to disregard it? How?

"You may have been mistaken, witness, as to the identity of the man you saw in London. It may not have been the Thorn you had known here."

Mr. Ebenezer James smiled a peculiar smile. "I was not mistaken," he said, his tone sounding remarkably significant. "I am upon my oath."

"Call Aphrodite Hallijohn."

The lady appeared, supported by her friend the policeman, and Mr. Ebenezer James was desired by Mr. Ball to leave the court while she gave her evidence. Doubtless he had his reasons.

"What is your name?"

"Afy," replied she, looking daggers at everybody and sedulously keeping her back turned upon Francis Levison and Otway Bethel.

"Your name in full, if you please. You were not christened 'Afy'?"

"Aphrodite Hallijohn. You all know my name as well as I do. Where's the use of asking useless questions?"

"Swear the witness," said Mr. Justice Hare.

"I won't be sworn," said Afy.

"You must be sworn," said Mr. Justice Herbert.

"But I say I won't," repeated Afy.

"Then we must commit you to prison for contempt of court."

There was no mercy in his tone, and Afy turned white. Sir John Dobede interposed.

"Young woman, had you a hand in the murder of your father?"

"I?" returned Afy, struggling with passion, temper, and excitement. "How dare you ask me so unnatural a question, sir? He was the kindest father!" she added, battling with her tears. "I loved him dearly. I would have saved his life with mine."

"And yet you refuse to give evidence that may assist in bringing his destroyer to justice!"

"No. I don't refuse on that score. I should like his destroyer to be hanged, and I'd go to see it. But who knows what other questions you may be asking me—about things that concern neither you nor anybody else? That's why I object."

"We have only to deal with what bears upon the murder. The questions put to you will relate to that."

Afy considered. "Well, you may swear me, then," she said. Little notion she had of the broad gauge those questions would run upon. And she was sworn accordingly. Very unwillingly yet. For Afy, who would have told lies by the bushel unsworn, did look upon an oath as a serious matter, and felt herself compelled to speak the truth when examined under it.

"How did you become acquainted with a gentleman you often saw in those days—Captain Thorn?"

"There!" uttered the dismayed Afy. "You are beginning already. He had nothing to do with it. He did not do the murder."

"You have sworn to answer the question put," was the uncompromising rejoinder. "How did you become acquainted with Captain Thorn?"

"I met him at Swainson," doggedly answered Afy. "I went over there one day just for a spree, and I met him at the pastry-cook's."

"And he fell in love with your pretty face?" said Lawyer Ball, taking up the examination.

In the incense to her vanity Afy nearly forgot her scruples. "Yes, he did," she answered, casting a smile of general fascination round upon the court.

"And got out of you where you lived and entered upon his courting, riding over nearly every evening to see you?"

"Well," acknowledged Afy, "there was no harm in it."

"Oh, certainly not," acquiesced the lawyer, in a pleasant, free tone, to put the witness at her ease. "Rather good, I should say. I wish I had the like luck. Did you know him at that time by the name of Levison?"

"No. He said he was Captain Thorn, and I thought he was."

"Did you know where he lived?"

"No. He never said that. I thought he was stopping temporarily at Swainson."

"And—dear me, what a sweet bonnet that is you have on?"

Afy—whose egregious vanity was her besetting sin, who possessed enough of it for any ten pretty women going—cast a glance out of the corners of her eyes at the admired bonnet, and became Mr. Ball's entirely.

"And how long was it, after your first meeting with him, before you discovered his real name?"

"Not for a long time. Several months."

"Subsequently to the murder, I presume?"

"Oh, yes."

Mr. Ball's eyes gave a twinkle, and unconscious Afy surreptitiously smoothed with one finger the glossy parting of her hair.

"Besides Captain Thorn, what gentlemen were in the wood the night of the murder?"

"Richard Hare was there. Otway Bethel and Locksley also. Those were all I saw—until the crowd came."

"Were Locksley and Mr. Otway Bethel martyrs to your charms—as the other two were?"

"No, indeed," was the witness's answer, with an indignant toss of the head. "A couple of poaching fellows like them! They had better have tried it on!"

"Which of the two, Hare or Thorn, was inside the cottage with you that evening?"

Afy came out of her vanity and hesitated. She was beginning to wonder where the questions would get to.

"You are upon your oath, witness!" thundered Mr. Justice Hare. "If it was my—if it was Richard Hare who was with you, say so. But there must be no equivocation here."

Afy was startled. "It was Thorn," she answered to Mr. Ball.

"And where was Richard Hare?"

"I don't know. He came down, but I sent him away, I would not admit him. I dare say he lingered in the wood."

"Did he leave a gun with you?"

"Yes. It was one he had promised to lend my father. I put it down just inside the door, he told me it was loaded."

"How long after this was it before your father interrupted you?"

"He didn't interrupt us at all," returned Afy. "I never saw my father until I saw him dead."

"Were you not in the cottage all the time?"

"No. We went out for a stroll at the back. Captain Thorn wished me goodbye there, and I stayed out."

"Did you hear the gun go off?"

"I heard a shot as I was sitting on the stump of a tree and thinking. But I attached no importance to it, never supposing it was in the cottage."

"What was it that Captain Thorn had to get from the cottage after he quitted you? What had he left there?"

Now this was a random shaft. Lawyer Ball, a keen man, who had well weighed all points in the tale imparted to him by Richard Hare, as well as other points, had made his own deductions, and spoke accordingly. Afy was taken in.

"He had left his hat there, nothing else. It was a warm evening, and he had gone out without it."

"He told you, I believe, sufficient to convince you of the guilt of Richard Hare?" Another shaft thrown at random.

"I did not want convincing. I knew it without. Everybody else knew it."

"To be sure," equably returned Lawyer Ball. "Did Captain Thorn see it done—and did he tell you that?"

"He had got his hat and was away down in the wood some little distance when he heard voices in dispute in the cottage, and recognized one of them to be that of my father. The shot followed close upon it, and he guessed some mischief had been done, though he did not suspect its extent."

"Thorn told you this? When?"

"The same night. Much later."

"How came you to see him?"

Afy hesitated. But she was sternly told to answer the question.

"A boy came up to the cottage and called me out, and said a strange gentleman wanted to see me in the wood, and had given him sixpence to come for me. I went, and found Captain Thorn. He asked what the commotion was about, and I told him Richard Hare had killed my father. He said that, now I spoke of him, he could recognize Richard Hare's as having been the other voice in the dispute."

"What boy was that—the one who came for you?"

"It was Mother Whiteman's little son."

"And Captain Thorn then gave you this version of the tragedy?"

"It was the right version," resentfully spoke Afy.

"How do you know that?"

"Oh, because I'm sure it was. Who else would kill him but Richard Hare? It was a scandalous shame, your wanting to put it upon Thorn."

"Look at the prisoner, Sir Francis Levison. Is it he whom you knew as Thorn?"

"Yes. But that does not make him guilty of the murder."

"Of course it does not," complacently assented Lawyer Ball. "How long did you remain with Captain Thorn in London—upon that little visit, you know?"

Afy stared like anybody moonstruck.

"When you quitted this place after the tragedy it was to join Captain Thorn in London. How long, I ask, did you remain with him?" Entirely a random shaft this.

"Who says I was with him? Who says I went after him?"

"I do," replied Lawyer Ball, taking note of her confusion. "Come, it's over and done with. It's no use to deny it now. We all go upon visits to friends sometimes."

"I never heard anything so bold!" cried Afy. "Where will you tell me I went next?"

"You are upon your oath, woman!" again interposed Justice Hare, and a trembling, as of agitation, might be detected in his voice, in spite of its ringing severity. "Were you with the prisoner, Levison, or were you with Richard Hare?"

"I with Richard Hare!" cried Afy, agitated in her turn, and shaking like an aspen leaf, partly with discomfiture, partly with an unknown dread. "How dare that cruel falsehood be brought up again to my face? I never saw Richard Hare after the night of the murder. I swear it. I swear that I have never seen him since. Visit him! I'd sooner visit Calcraft, the hangman."

There was truth in the words, in the tone. The chairman let fall the hand which had been raised to his face, holding on his eyeglasses, and a sort of self-condemning fear arose, confusing his brain. His son proved innocent of one part might be proved innocent of the other, and then how would his own harsh conduct show out? West Lynne, in its charity, the justice, in his, had cast more odium to Richard with regard to his after conduct touching this girl than it had on the score of the murder.

"Come," said Lawyer Ball, in a coaxing tone. "Let us be pleasant. Of course you were not with Richard Hare. West Lynne is always ill-natured. You were only on a visit to Captain Thorn, as—as any other young lady might be?"

Afy hung her head, cowed down to abject meekness.

"Answer the question," came forth the chairman's voice again. "Were you with Thorn?"

"Yes." Though the answer was feeble enough.

Mr. Ball coughed an insinuating cough. "Did you remain with him—say, two or three years?"

"Not three."

"A little over two, perhaps?"

"There was no harm in it!" shrieked Afy with a catching sob of temper. "If I chose to live in London, and he chose to make a morning call upon me now and then as an old friend, what's that to anybody? Where was the harm, I ask?"

"Certainly—where was the harm? I am not insinuating any," returned Lawyer Ball, with a wink of the eye furthest from the witness bench. "And, during the time that—that he was making these little morning calls upon you did you know him to be Levison?"

"Yes. I knew him to be Captain Levison then."

"Did he ever tell you why he assumed the name of Thorn?"

"'Only for a whim,' he said. The day he spoke to me in the pastry-cook's shop at Swainson something came over him in the spur of the moment not to give the right name, so he gave the first that come into his head. He never thought to retain it, or that other people would hear of him by it."

"I dare say not," said Lawyer Ball, dryly. "Well, Miss Afy, I believe that is all for the present. I want Ebenezer James in again," he whispered to an officer of the justice-room, as the witness retired.

Ebenezer James reappeared and took Afy's place. "You informed their worships just now that you had met Thorn in London some eighteen months subsequent to the murder," began Lawyer Ball, launching another of his shafts. "This must have been during Afy Hallijohn's sojourn with him. Did you also see her?"

Mr. Ebenezer opened his eyes. He knew nothing of the evidence just given by Afy, and wondered how on earth it had come out—that she had been with Thorn at all. He had never betrayed it. "Afy?" stammered he.

"Yes, Afy," sharply returned the lawyer. "Their worships know that when she left West Lynne it was to join Thorn, not Richard Hare—though the latter has borne the credit of it. I ask you did you see her? For she was then still connected with him."

"Well—yes, I did," replied Mr. Ebenezer, his own scruples removed, but wondering still how it had been discovered; unless Afy had, as he had half prophesied she would—let it out in her "tantrums." "In fact, it was Afy whom I first saw."

"State the circumstances."

"I was up Paddington way one afternoon, and saw a lady going into a house. It was Afy Hallijohn. She lived there, I found—had the drawing room apartments. She invited me to stay to tea with her, and I did."

"Did you see Captain Levison there?"

"I saw Thorn—as I thought him to be. Afy told me I must be away by eight o'clock, for she was expecting a friend, who sometimes came to sit with her for an hour's chat. But in talking over old times—not that I could tell her much about West Lynne, for I had left it almost as long as she had—the time slipped on past the hour. When Afy found that out, she hurried me off, and I had barely got outside the gate when a cab drove up, and Thorn alighted from it, and let himself in with a latch-key. That is all I know."

"When you knew that the scandal of Afy's absence rested on Richard Hare why could you not have said this, and cleared him on your return to West Lynne?"

"It was no affair of mine that I should make it public. Afy asked me not to say I had seen her, and I promised her I would not. As to

Richard Hare, a little scandal on his back was nothing, while there remained on it the worse scandal of the murder."

"Stop a bit," interposed Mr. Rubiny, as the witness was about to retire. "You speak of the time being eight o'clock in the evening, sir. Was it dark?"

"Yes."

"Then how could you be certain it was Thorn who got out of the cab and entered?"

"I am quite certain. There was a gas lamp right at the spot, and I saw him as well as I should have seen him in daylight. I knew his voice, too; could have sworn to it anywhere. And I could almost have sworn to him by his splendid diamond ring. It flashed in the lamplight."

"His voice! Did he speak to you?"

"No. But he spoke to the cabman. There was a half dispute between them. The man said Thorn had not paid him enough, that he had not allowed for the having kept him waiting twenty minutes on the road. Thorn swore at him a bit, and then flung him an extra shilling."

The next witness was a man who had been groom to the late Sir Peter Levison. He testified that the prisoner, Francis Levison, had been on a visit to his master late in the summer and part of the autumn the year that Hallijohn was killed. That he frequently rode out in the direction of West Lynne, especially toward evening; would be away for three or four hours, and come home with the horse in a foam. Also that he picked up two letters at different times which Mr. Levison had carelessly let fall from his pocket, and returned them to him. Both the notes were addressed "Captain Thorn." But they had not been through the post, for there was no further superscription on them, and the writing looked like a lady's. He remembered quite well hearing of the murder of Hallijohn, the witness added, in answer to a question; it made a great stir throughout the country. It was just at that same time that Mr. Levison concluded his visit and returned to London.

"A wonderful memory!" Mr. Rubiny sarcastically remarked.

The witness, a quite respectable man, replied that he had a good memory, but that circumstances had impressed upon it particularly the fact that Mr. Levison's departure followed close upon the murder of Hallijohn.

"What circumstances?" demanded the bench.

"One day when Sir Peter was round at the stables, gentlemen, he was urging his nephew to prolong his visit, and asked what sudden freak was taking him off. Mr. Levison replied that unexpected business called him to London. While they were talking the coachman came up, all in a heat, telling that Hallijohn, of West Lynne, had been murdered by young Mr. Hare. I remember Sir Peter said he could not believe it, and that it must have been an accident, not murder."

"Is this all?"

"There was more said. Mr. Levison, in a shamed-faced sort of manner, asked his uncle would he let him have five or ten pounds? Sir Peter seemed angry, and asked what he had done with the fifty-pound note he had made him a present of only the previous morning? Mr. Levison replied that he had sent that away in a letter to a brother officer to whom he was in debt. Sir Peter refused to believe it, and said he was more likely to have squandered it upon some disgraceful folly. Mr. Levison denied that he had, but he looked confused; indeed, his manner was altogether confused that morning."

"Did he get the five or ten pounds?"

"I don't know, gentlemen. I dare say he did, for my master was as persuadable as a woman, though he'd fly out a bit sometimes at first. Mr. Levison departed for London that same night."

The last witness called was Mr. Dill. On the previous Tuesday evening he had been returning home from spending an hour at Mr. Beauchamp's, when, in the field opposite to Mr. Justice Hare's, he suddenly heard a commotion. It arose from the meeting of Sir Francis Levison and Otway Bethel. The former appeared to have been enjoying a solitary moonlight ramble, and the latter to have encountered him unexpectedly. Words ensued. Bethel accused Sir Francis of "shirking" him; Sir Francis answered angrily that he knew nothing of him, and nothing he wanted to know.

"You were glad enough to know something of me the night of Hallijohn's murder," retorted Bethel to this. "Do you remember that I could hang you? One little word from me, and you would stand in Dick Hare's place."

"You fool!" passionately cried Sir Francis. "You could not hang me without putting your own head in the noose. Had you not your hush-money? Are you wanting to do me out of more?"

"A cursed paltry note of fifty pounds?" foamed Otway Bethel, "which many a time since I have wished my fingers had been blown off before they touched. I never should have touched it, but that I was altogether overwhelmed with the moment's confusion. I have not been able to look Mrs. Hare in the face since—knowing I hold the secret that would save her son from the hangman."

"And put yourself in his place," sneered Sir Francis.

"No. Put you."

"That's as it might be. But if I went to the hangman you would go with me. There would be no excuse or escape for you. You know it."

The warfare continued longer, but this was the cream of it. Mr. Dill heard the whole, and repeated it now to the magistrates. Mr. Rubiny protested that it was "inadmissible," "hearsay evidence," "contrary to law," but the bench oracularly put Mr. Rubiny down, and told him they did not require any stranger to come there and teach them their business.

Colonel Bethel had leaned forward at the conclusion of Mr. Dill's evidence, dismay on his face, agitation in his voice. "Are you sure that you made no mistake? That the other in this interview was Otway Bethel?"

Mr. Dill sadly shook his head. "Am I one to swear to a wrong man, colonel? I wish I had not heard it—save that it may be the means of clearing Richard Hare."

Sir Francis Levison had braved out the proceedings with a haughty cavalier air, his delicate hands and his diamond ring remarkably conspicuous. Was that stone the real thing, or a false one substituted for the real? Hard up as he had long been for money, the suspicion might arise. A derisive smile crossed his features at parts of the evidence, as much as to say you may convict me as to Mademoiselle Afy, but you can not as to the murder. When, however, Mr. Dill's testimony was given, what a change was there! His mood tamed down to what looked like abject fear.

"Of course your worship will take bail for Sir Francis," said Mr. Rubiny at the close of the proceedings.

Bail! The bench looked at one another.

"Your worship will not refuse it—a gentleman in Sir Francis Levison's position!"

The bench thought they never had so insolent an application

made to them. Bail for him—on this charge! No; not if the lord chancellor himself came down to offer it.

Mr. Otway Bethel, conscious, probably, that nobody would offer bail for him, not even the colonel, did not ask the bench to take it. So the two were fully committed to take their trial for the "willful murder, otherwise the killing and slaying of George Hallijohn."

And that vain, ill-starred Afy? What of her? Well, Afy had again retired to the witness room after giving evidence, and there she remained till the close, agreeably occupied in a mental debate. What would they make out from her admission regarding her sojourn in London and the morning calls? How would that precious West Lynne construe it? She did not much care; she would brave it out, and assail them with towering indignation did any care to cast a stone at her.

Such was her final decision, arrived at just as the proceedings terminated. Afy was right glad to remain where she was till some of the bustle had gone.

"How has it ended?" she asked of Mr. Ball, who, being a bachelor, was ever regarded with much graciousness by Afy, for she kept her eyes open to contingencies, although Mr. Joe Jiffin was held as a reserve.

"They are both committed for willful murder. Off to Lynne-borough in an hour."

Afy's color rose. "What a shame! To commit two innocent men upon such a charge!"

"I can tell you what, Miss Afy, the sooner you disabuse your mind of that prejudice the better. Levison has been as good as proved guilty today; but if proof were wanting he and Bethel have criminated each other. 'When rogues fall out honest men get their own.' Not that I can quite fathom Bethel's share in the exploit, though I can pretty well guess at it. And in proving themselves guilty they have proved the innocence of Richard Hare!"

Afy's face was changing to whiteness; her confident air to one of dread; her vanity to humiliation.

"It—can't—be—true!" she gasped.

"It's true enough. The part you have hitherto ascribed to Thorn was enacted by Richard Hare. He heard the shot from his place in the wood, and saw Thorn run, ghastly, trembling, horrified, from his wicked work. Believe me, it was Thorn who killed your father."

Afy grew cold as she listened. That one awful moment, when conviction that his words were true forced itself upon her, was enough to sober her for a whole lifetime. Thorn! Her sight failed; her head reeled; her very heart turned to sickness. One struggling cry of pain, and Afy Hallijohn fell forward in a fainting fit.

Shouts, hisses, execrations, yells! The prisoners were being brought forth to be conveyed to Lynneborough. A whole posse of constables were necessary to protect them against the outbreak of the mob, which outbreak was not directed against Otway Bethel, but against Sir Francis Levison. Cowering, like the guilty culprit that he was, he shivered, and hid his white face, wondering whether it would be a repetition of Justice Hare's green pond, into which he had been tossed already, or the tearing of him asunder piecemeal, and cursing the earth because it did not open and let him in!

Police-Sergeant Reading's Clue

From *The Notting Hill Mystery*

CHARLES FELIX

The author of *The Notting Hill Mystery* (1862) is unknown, although it has been attributed to an otherwise obscure writer named Charles Felix. The name suggests a pseudonym, but it is not known of whom. Felix is credited with one other novel, not a mystery. Appearing two years after *The Woman in White, The Notting Hill Mystery* borrows the technique Collins was perfecting, and uses statements, letters, and other documents to elucidate a case of triple murder. The prose is lean, the pace swift, and the style peculiarly modern in flavor.

In the short excerpt here, a police sergeant makes excellent use of the deductive method to uncover some vital pieces of evidence that point toward a murderer other than the one in custody. In its own way, the novel anticipates the style, the methods, and the pacing of *The Moonstone*.

I am a sergeant on the detective staff of the Metropolitan Police. In October, 1856, I was on duty at Notting Hill. I was employed to watch a gentleman by the name of Anderton. He was in custody on a coroner's warrant for the murder of his lady, but couldn't be removed on account of being ill. I was put in the house to prevent his escape.

I did not stay in his room. I did at first, but it seemed of no use; so

I spoke to our superintendent, and got leave from him to stop in the outer-room. I did this to make things pleasant. I always try to make things as pleasant as I can, compatible with duty, specially when it's a gentleman. It comes harder on them than on the regular hands, because they are not so much used to it.

In this case the prisoner seemed to take on terribly. He was very weak and ill—too weak seemingly to get out of bed. He used to lie with his eyes fixed upon one corner of the room, muttering sometimes to himself, but I couldn't tell what. He never spoke to anyone. The only time he spoke was once, to ask me to let him see the body [of his wife]. I hadn't the heart to say no; but I went with him, and kept at the door. He could hardly totter along, he was so weakly.

After about half an hour, I thought it was all very quiet, and looked in. He was lying on the floor in a dead faint, and I carried him back. He never spoke again, but lay just as I have said. Of course I took every precaution. Prisoner's room had two doors, one opening on the landing, and the other into the room where I stopped.

I locked up the outer-door and put three or four screws into it from the outside. The window was too high to break out at, but our men used to keep an eye on it from the street. At night I used to lock the door of my room and stick open the door between the two. I was relieved occasionally by Sergeant Walsh, but I mostly preferred seeing to it myself. I like to keep my own work in my own hands, and this was a very interesting case.

When I first took charge I made a careful examination of the premises and of all papers, and the like. I found nothing to criminate the prisoner. I found a journal of the lady who was murdered, with a note at the end in his hand-writing; but so far as it went they seemed to be on very good terms.

I found also a lot of prescriptions and notes referring to her illness, but no papers like that found by the nurse [this paper had "Tartar Emetic" printed on it, with the word "Poison" written underneath. Tartar Emetic was the poison suspected of having killed Anderton's wife], nor any traces of powders or drugs of any kind. I went with the nurse into the bedroom of the murdered party, and made her point out the exact spot where the paper was found.

According to what she said it was lying just under the bed on the right hand side. The glove was lying close to it, but not under the bed.

Somehow I didn't quite feel as if it was all on the square. I thought the business of the paper looked rather queer. It didn't seem quite feasible like. I have known a thing of that sort by way of a plant before now, so I thought I'd just go on asking questions. That's always my way. I ask all kinds of questions about everything, feeling my way like. I generally find something turn up that way before I have done.

Something turned up this time. I don't know that it was much—perhaps not. I have my own opinion about that. This is how it was. After more questions of one kind or another, I got to something that led me to ask the nurse which side of the bed Mr. Anderton usually went to give the lady food and physic. She and the other servants all agreed that, being naturally left-handed, like, he always went to the *left* hand side of the bed, so as he could get to feed her with a spoon. He was very bad with his right hand. Couldn't handle a spoon with it no more than some of us would with the left. Nurse said she had seen him try once or twice, which he always spilled everything. I mean of course with his right hand. He was handy enough with his left.

When I heard this I began to suspect we might be on a false scent. This is the way I looked at it. The glove, as I told you, was lying on the floor by the right side of the bed, so as anybody who dropped it must have been standing on that side which it's the natural side to go to as being nearest the door. The paper was close to it, just under the same side of the bed.

Now I took it as pretty clear the prisoner hadn't put the paper there for the purpose, but if he'd done it at all, he had dropped it by accident in giving the stuff. I fancy, too, he'd naturally be particularly careful in giving that sort of stuff not to spill it about the place, so he'd be pretty well sure to take his best hand to it. In that case he'd have dropped it on the left hand side of the bed—not the right.

Still, of course, it might have got blown across, or, for the matter of that, kicked, though that was not very likely, as the bed was a wide one, and put in a sort of recess like, quite out of any sort of draught.

So I thought I'd have another look at the place, and, poking about under the bed, I found a long narrow box, which the servants told me was full of bows and arrows, and hadn't been moved out of its place since they first came to the house. It took up the whole length of the bed within a foot or so, and lay right along the middle on the floor. There was a mark along the floor that showed how long it had been there.

A bit of paper like that could never have got blown right over that without touching it if there had been ever such a draught. When I'd got so far, I fancied things began to look very queer, so I got the bed shifted out of its place altogether. The coffin was in the way, and I got that moved to one side of the room, and pulled the bed right clear of the box.

As we shifted the coffin I thought I saw some thing like a piece of paper under the flannel shroud. I said nothing at the time, but waited until the undertaker's men were out of the room and I was alone. I then opened the shroud and found a small folded paper. It was put just under the hands, which were crossed over the bosom of the corpse. I opened it and found a lock of hair, which I saw directly was Mr. Anderton's, and there were a few words in writing which I copied down in my notebook, and then I put the hair and the paper and all back where I found them. The writing was: "Pray for me, darling, pray for me." I knew the hand at once for Mr. Anderton's. His writing is very remarkable, by reason, I suppose, of being so left-handed.

Of course that wasn't evidence, but somehow I got an idea out of it that a man wouldn't go on in that way with his wife just after he'd been and murdered her. It struck me that that would be against nature, leastways if he was in his right mind.

After I had finished with the coffin I took a look at the box. As I expected, the top was covered ever so thick with dust, and it was pretty clear that, at all events, the bit of paper had never lain atop of it. I put a piece just like it on to try and blew it off again, and it made a quite great mark and got all dirty. The paper picked up by the nurse was quite clean, or very nearly so.

Putting all this together I came pretty nigh a conclusion that, at all events, it wasn't Mr. Anderton as had dropped the paper there. The sides of the box were also dusty, but there were marks on them like as if a brush or a broom had brushed against them.

I put the box and the bed back into their places, and went down to question the housemaid. I found that she had put the room tidy the day Mrs. Anderton died and had passed a short hair-broom under the bed as there were several things lying about. She said she was quite sure there was no bit of paper there then, as she had stooped down and looked under. I tried with the same broom, and you couldn't reach the box without stooping, as she said.

I then inquired who had been in the room between the time of the death and the finding of the paper. No one had been there but the nurse, the doctor, and housemaid, and Baron R**. I was determined to hunt it out if possible.

I questioned the nurse and the housemaid—on the quiet, not to excite suspicion—but felt pretty clear they knew nothing more about it; and when next Baron R** came I sounded him about different points. He did not seem to know that Mr. Anderton was so left-handed, nor could I get any information from him on the subject. He didn't seem at first to see what I was driving at, and, of course, I didn't mean he should, but after a while I saw he had struck out the same idea as I had about the place where the paper was found, though I had not meant to let him in to that.

He seemed quite struck of a heap by it. I fancied at the moment that he turned regularly pale, but he was just blowing his nose with a large yellow silk handkerchief, and I could not be sure. He said nothing to me of what he had guessed, nor did I to him. I like to keep those things as quiet as I can, particularly from parties' friends. I have not been able to get any further clue, but I am convinced that something is to be made of that paper business yet. I generally know a scent when I get on one, and my notion is that I am on one now.

Footprints
in the Snow

From *Monsieur Lecoq*

EMILE GABORIAU

Translated from the original French

Emile Gaboriau (1835–1873) is credited with the creation of the French *roman-policier* (police novel) during the 1860s, a genre that combines the detective skills of Vidocq with the romantic skills of Alexandre Dumas. In effect, the police novel is a first cousin to the detective novel. *Monsieur Lecoq* (1869) provides a sustained, suspenseful, and careful exposition of deductive reasoning—and its explanation—by the protagonist to an admiring pre-Watson Watson, who at one point exclaims to Lecoq, "Wonderful! Prodigious!" about a complicated explanation of deductive reasoning. Later Lecoq modestly comments, "Nonsense. What have I done that is so clever?"

The police novel, with its usual lengthy flashback, like a dossier attached to a progress report, is not *totally* concerned with detection. In this excerpt from *Monsieur Lecoq*, three men have been killed in a barroom brawl, and a suspect arrested by Inspector Gevrol. Gevrol leaves Monsieur Lecoq, a young policeman, and his assistant, "Father" Absinthe, a veteran fond of his booze, in charge until the commissioner arrives. Lecoq thinks the suspect innocent, and begins a Socratic dialogue with his companion.

"Whom do you suppose the person we have just arrested to be?"

"A porter, probably, or a vagabond."

"That is to say, a man belonging to the lowest order of society; consequently, a man without education."

"Certainly."

"What would you say," Lecoq continued, "if I should prove to you that this young man had received an excellent, even refined education?"

"I should reply that it was very extraordinary. I should reply that—but what a fool I am! You have not proved it to me yet."

"But I can do so very easily. Do you remember the words that he uttered as he fell?"

"Yes, I remember them perfectly. He said: 'It is the Prussians who are coming.'"

"What a question! I should suppose that he did not like Prussians, and that he supposed he was offering us a terrible insult."

Lecoq was waiting anxiously for this response.

"Ah, well! Father Absinthe," he said, gravely, "you are wrong, quite wrong. And that this man has an education superior to his apparent position is proved by the fact that you did not understand his meaning, nor his intention. It was this single phrase that made the case clear to me."

The physiognomy of Father Absinthe expressed the strange and comical perplexity of a man who is so thoroughly mystified that he knows not whether to laugh or be angry. After reflecting a little, he decided to be angry.

"You are rather too young to impose upon an old man like me," he remarked. "I do not like boasters—"

"One moment!" interrupted Lecoq; "allow me to explain. You have certainly heard of a terrible battle which resulted in one of the greatest defeats that ever happened to France—the battle of Waterloo?"

"I do not see the connection—"

"Answer, if you please."

"Yes—then!"

"Very well; you must know, then, papa, that for some time victory perched upon the banners of France. The English began to fall back, and already the emperor exclaimed: 'We have them!' when suddenly on the right a little in the rear, troops were seen advancing. It was the Prussian army. The battle of Waterloo was lost."

In all his life, worthy Father Absinthe had never made such strenuous efforts to understand anything. In this case they were not wholly useless, for he half rose in his chair, and with the tone in which Archimedes cried "I have found it!" he exclaimed:

"I understand. The man's words were only an allusion."

"It is as you have said," remarked Lecoq, approvingly. "But I had not finished. If the emperor was thrown into consternation by the appearance of the Prussians, it was because he was momentarily expecting the arrival of one of his own generals from the same direction—Grouchy—with thirty-five thousand men. So if this man's allusion was exact and complete, he was not expecting an enemy, but a friend. Now draw your own conclusions."

Amazed, but convinced, his companion opened to their widest extent the eyes that had been heavy with sleep a few moments before.

"*Mon Dieu!*" he murmured, "if you put it in that way! But I forget; you must have seen something, as you were looking through the cracks of the shutter."

The young man shook his head.

"Upon my honor," he declared, "I saw nothing save the struggle between the murderer and the poor devil in the garb of a soldier. It was that sentence alone that aroused my attention."

"Wonderful! prodigious!" exclaimed the astonished old man.

"I will add that reflection has confirmed my suspicions. I asked myself why this man, instead of fleeing, should have waited and remained there, at that door, to parley with us."

With a bound, Father Absinthe was upon his feet.

"Why?" he interrupted; "because he had accomplices, and he wished to give them time to escape. Ah! I understand it all now."

A triumphant smile parted Lecoq's lips.

"That is what I said to myself," he replied; "and now it is easy to verify my suspicions. There is snow outside, is there not?"

It was not necessary to say any more. The elder officer seized the light, and followed by his companion, he hastened to the back door of the house, which opened into a small garden.

In this sheltered enclosure the snow had not melted, and upon its white surface numerous footprints lay, like dark stains.

Without hesitation, Lecoq threw himself upon his knees in the snow, in order to examine them; he rose again almost immediately.

"These indentations were not made by the feet of men," said he. "There have been women here."

"A fine affair!" exclaimed Father Absinthe; "an excellent case!" And suddenly recollecting a maxim that has been handed down from the time of Cicero, he added, in sententious tones: "Who holds the woman holds the cause!"

Lecoq did not deign to reply. He was standing upon the threshold, leaning against the casing of the door, his hand pressed to his forehead, as motionless as a statue.

The presence of two men in this vile den explained everything in the most natural and common-place fashion. Their presence explained the quarrel, the testimony of Widow Chupin [owner of the saloon], the dying declaration of the pretended soldier.

The behavior of the murderer was also explained. He had remained to cover the retreat of the two women; he had sacrificed himself in order to save them, an act of that chivalrous gallantry so common in the French character, that even the scoundrels of the *barrières* were not entirely destitute of it.

But the strange allusion to the battle of Waterloo remained unexplained. While Lecoq was turning and twisting all these probabilities in his mind, Father Absinthe became impatient.

"Are we going to remain here until doomsday?" he asked. "Are we to pause just at the moment when our search has been productive of such brilliant results?"

"Brilliant results!" These words stung the young man's soul as deeply as the keenest irony could have done.

"Leave me alone," he replied gruffly; "and above all, do not walk about the garden. You will spoil the footprints."

His companion swore a little; then he, too, became silent. He submitted to the irresistible ascendancy of a superior will and intelligence.

Lecoq was engaged in following out his course of reasoning. "These are probably the events as they occurred," he thought.

"The murderer, leaving the ball at the Rainbow, a public house not far from here, near the fortifications, came to this saloon, accompanied by two women. He found three men drinking here, who either began teasing him, or who displayed too much gallantry to his companions. He became angry. The others threatened him; he was one against three; he was armed; he became wild with rage and fired—"

He checked himself, and in an instant after he added, aloud:

"But was it the murderer who brought these women here? If he is tried, this will be the important point. It is necessary to obtain information on the subject."

He immediately went back into the house, closely followed by his colleague, and began an examination of the footprints about the door that [Inspector] Gevrol had forced open.

Labor lost. There was but little snow on the ground about the entrance of the hovel, and so many persons had passed in and out that Lecoq could discover nothing.

Lecoq could have cried with rage. He saw the opportunity for which he had sighed so long indefinitely postponed. He fancied he could hear Gevrol's coarse sarcasms.

"Enough of this," he murmured, under his breath. "The general [Gevrol] was right, and I am a fool!"

He was so positively convinced that one could do no more than discover the circumstances of some commonplace, vulgar broil, that he began to wonder if it would not be wise to renounce his search and take a nap, while awaiting the coming of the commissioner of police.

But Father Absinthe was no longer of this opinion. This worthy man, who was far from suspecting the reflections in which his companion was indulging, could not explain his inaction.

"Ah, well! my boy," said he, "have you lost your wits? This is losing time, it seems to me. The justice will arrive in a few hours, and what report shall we present? As for me, if you desire to go to sleep, I shall pursue my investigations alone."

Disappointed as he was, the young police officer could not repress a smile. He recognized his own exhortations of a few moments before. It was the old man who had suddenly become intrepid.

"To work, then!" he sighed, like a man who, while foreseeing defeat, wishes, at least, to have no cause to reproach himself.

He found it, however, extremely difficult to follow the footprints in the open air by the uncertain light of a candle, which was extinguished by the least breath of wind.

"It is impossible," said Lecoq; "I wonder if there is not a lantern in the house. If we could only lay our hands upon it!"

They searched everywhere, and, at last, upstairs in the Widow

Chupin's own apartment, they found a well-trimmed lantern, so small and close that it certainly had never been intended for honest purposes.

"A regular burglar's implement," said Father Absinthe, with a coarse laugh.

The implement was useful in any case; the two men were agreed upon that when they returned to the garden and recommenced their investigations systematically.

They advanced very slowly and with extreme caution. The old man carefully held the lantern in the best position, and Lecoq, on his knees, studied each footprint with the attention of a chiromancer striving to read the future in the hand of a rich client.

A new examination assured Lecoq that he had been correct in his first supposition. It was plain that two women had quitted the building by this door. They had departed running; this was proved by the length of the steps and also by the shape of the footprints.

The difference in the tracks left by the two fugitives was so remarkable, that it did not escape Father Absinthe's eyes.

"*Cristi!*" he muttered; "one of these jades can boast of having a pretty foot at the end of her leg!"

He was right. One of the tracks betrayed a small, coquettish and slender foot, clad in an elegant high-heeled boot with a narrow sole and an arched instep.

The other denoted a broad, short foot, that grew wider toward the end, and which was encased in a strong, low shoe.

This was indeed a clew. Lecoq's hopes revived; so eagerly does a man welcome any supposition that is in accordance with his desires.

Trembling with anxiety, he went to examine other footprints a short distance from these; and an excited exclamation broke from his lips.

"What is it?" eagerly inquired the other agent; "what do you see?"

"Come and look for yourself, papa; see there."

The good man bent down, and his surprise was so great that he almost dropped the lantern.

"Oh!" said he, in a stifled voice, "a man's footprint!"

"Exactly. And this fellow wore the finest of boots. See that imprint, how clear, how neat it is!"

Worthy Father Absinthe was furiously scratching his ear, his usual method of quickening his rather slow wits.

"But it seems to me," he ventured at last, "that this individual was not coming *from* this ill-fated hovel."

"Of course not; the direction of the foot tells you that. No, he was not going from here, he was coming here. But he did not pass beyond the spot where we are now standing. He was advancing on tip-toe with outstretched neck and listening ears, when, on reaching this spot, he heard some noise; fear seized him, and he fled."

"Or, rather, the women were going out as he was coming, and—"

"No, the women were outside the garden when he entered it."

This assertion seemed far too audacious to suit Lecoq's companion, who remarked: "One cannot be sure of that."

"I am sure of it, however; and can prove it conclusively. You doubt it, papa? It is because your eyes are growing old. Bring your lantern a little nearer—yes, here it is—our man placed his large foot upon one of the marks made by the woman with the small foot and has almost effaced it."

This unexceptionable bit of circumstantial evidence stupefied the old policeman.

"Now," continued Lecoq, "could this man have been the accomplice whom the murderer was expecting? Might it not have been some strolling vagrant whose attention was attracted by the two pistol shots? This is what we must ascertain. And we will ascertain it. Come!"

A wooden fence of lattice-work, a trifle more than three feet high, similar to that which prevents access to the railway trains, was all that separated the Widow Chupin's garden from the waste land that surrounded it.

When Lecoq made the circuit of the house to cut off the escape of the murderer, he had encountered this obstacle, and, fearing lest he should arrive too late, he had leaped the barrier, to the great detriment of his pantaloons, without even asking if there were not a gateway.

One did exist, however. A light gate of lattice-work similar to the fence, turning upon iron hinges and kept closed by a wooden button, allowed one to enter or depart from this side of the garden.

It was straight to this gate that these footprints in the snow led the two policemen.

Some new thought must have struck the younger man, for he paused suddenly.

"Ah!" he murmured, "these two women did not come to

Poivière this evening for the first time."

"Why do you think that, my boy?" inquired Father Absinthe.

"I could almost swear it. How, unless they were in the habit of coming to this den, could they have been aware of the existence of this gate? Could they have discovered it this dark and foggy night? No; for I, who can, without boasting, say that I have good eyes—I did not see it."

"Ah! yes, that is true!"

"These two women, however, came here without hesitating, without diverging from a straight line; and note that to do this, it was necessary for them to cross the garden diagonally."

The veteran would have given something if he could have found some objection to offer; but unfortunately he could find none.

"Upon my word!" he exclaimed, "yours is a droll way of proceeding. You are only a conscript; I am a veteran in the service, and have assisted in more affairs of this sort than you are years old, but never have I seen—"

"Nonsense!" interrupted Lecoq; "you will see much more. For example, I can prove to you that, although the women knew the exact position of the gate, the man knew it only by hearsay."

"The proof!"

"The fact is easily demonstrated, papa. Study the man's footprints, and you, who are very sharp, will see at once that he deviated greatly from the straight course. He was in such doubt, that he was obliged to search for the gate with his hand stretched out before him—and his fingers have left their imprint on the thin covering of snow that lies upon the upper railing of the fence."

The old man would have been glad to verify this statement for himself, as he said; but Lecoq was in a hurry.

"Let us go on, let us go on!" said he. "You can verify my assertions some other time."

They left the garden and followed the footprints that led them toward the outer boulevards, inclining a little to the right in the direction of the Rue de Patay.

Now there was no longer any need of close attention. No one, save the fugitive, had crossed this lonely waste since the last fall of snow. A child could have followed the track, so clear and distinct was it.

Four impressions, very unlike in character, formed the track;

two were those left by the women; the other two, one going and one returning, had been made by the man.

On several occasions the latter had placed his foot exactly on the footprints left by the two women, half effacing them, thus doing away with all doubts as to the precise moment in which he had come.

About a hundred yards from the Poivrière, Lecoq suddenly seized his colleague's arm.

"Halt!" he commanded; "we have reached a good place; I can see unmistakable proofs."

The spot was an abandoned lumber-yard, or rather a reservation belonging to a boat-builder. The ground was strewn with large blocks of granite, some chiselled, some in the rough, and with many long planks and logs of wood.

Before one of these planks, whose surface had evidently been wiped off, all these footprints came together, mingling confusedly.

"Here," declared the young detective, "our fugitives met this man and took counsel with him. One of the women, the one with the little feet, sat down upon this log."

"We should assure ourselves of this more fully," said Father Absinthe, in an oracular tone.

But his companion cut short these desires for verification.

"You—my old friend," said he, "are going to do me the kindness to keep perfectly still; pass me the lantern and do not move."

Lecoq's modest tone had suddenly become so imperious that his colleague dared offer no resistance.

Like a soldier at the command to halt, he remained erect, motionless and mute, following the movements of his friend with a curious and wondering eye.

Quick in his motions, and understanding how to maneuver the lantern in accordance with his wishes, the young policeman explored the surroundings in a very short space of time.

A bloodhound in pursuit of his prey would have been less alert, less discerning, less agile than he.

He came and went, turned, came back again, hurried on, or paused without any apparent reason; he scrutinized, he questioned everything; the earth, the logs of wood, the blocks of stone, and even the most insignificant objects; sometimes standing, but oftener on his knees, sometimes flat upon his belly, his face so near the ground that his breath must have melted the snow.

He had drawn a tape-line from his pocket: he used it with a carpenter's dexterity, and measured, measured, measured.

And all these movements were accompanied with the wild gestures of a madman, interspersed with oaths or short laughs, with exclamations of disappointment or of delight.

After a quarter of an hour of this strange exercise, he returned to Father Absinthe, placed the lantern on a stone, wiped his hands on his pocket-handkerchief, and said:

"Now I know all."

"Well, that is saying a great deal!"

"When I say all, I mean all that is connected with this episode of the drama which ended in blood in that hovel there. This expanse of earth, covered with snow, is an immense white page upon which the people we are in search of have written, not only their movements and their goings and comings, but their secret thoughts, the hopes and anxieties that agitated them. What do these footprints say to you, papa? To me they are as much alive as the persons who made them; they breathe, they speak, they accuse!"

The old officer was saying to himself:

"Certainly, this fellow is intelligent; undeniably, he is shrewd; but he is very disagreeable."

"These," pursued Lecoq, "are the facts as I have read them. When the murderer repaired to the Poivriére with the two women, his companion—I should call him his accomplice—came here to wait. He was a man of middle age and tall, wore a soft hat and a shaggy brown overcoat, was probably married, as he had a wedding-ring on the little finger of his right hand—"

The despairing gestures of his companion obliged the speaker to pause.

This description of a person whose existence had but just now been demonstrated, these precise details given in a tone of absolute certainty, overturned all of Father Absinthe's ideas completely, and increased his perplexity.

"This is not well," he growled; "this is not kind. You are making fun at me. I take the thing seriously; I listen to you, I obey you in everything, and this is the way you mock me. We find a clew, and instead of following it up, you stop to relate all these absurd stories."

"No," replied his companion, "I am not jesting, and I have told you nothing of which I am not absolutely sure—nothing—is not strictly and indisputably true."

"And you would have me believe—"

"Fear nothing, papa; I would not have you do violence to your convictions. When I have told you my reasons, and my means of information, you will laugh at the simplicity of the theory that seems so incomprehensible to you now."

"Go on, then," said the old man, in a tone of resignation.

"We had decided, my friend, that the accomplice mounted guard here. The time seemed long, and in order to relieve his impatience, he paced to and fro the length of this log of wood, and occasionally paused in his monotonous promenade to listen. Hearing nothing, he stamped his foot, doubtless exclaiming: 'What the devil has happened to him down there!' He had made about thirty turns (I have counted them), when a sound broke the stillness—the two women were coming."

On hearing Lecoq's recital, all the conflicting sentiments that are awakened in a child's mind by a fairy tale—doubt, faith, anxiety, and hope—filled Father Absinthe's heart.

What should he believe? what should he refuse to believe? He did not know. How was he to tell the true from the false among all these equally surprising assertions?

On the other hand, the gravity of his companion, which certainly was not feigned, dismissed all idea of pleasantry.

Then curiosity began to torture him.

"We had reached the point where the women made their appearance," said he.

"*Mon Dieu*! yes," responded Lecoq; "but here all certainty ceases; no more proofs, only suppositions. Still, I have every reason to believe that our fugitives left the drinking saloon before the beginning of the fight, before the cries that attracted our attention. Who were they? I can only conjecture. I suspect, however, that they were not equals in rank. I am inclined to think that one was the mistress, the other her servant."

"That one is proved," ventured the older man, "by the great difference in their feet and in their shoes."

This shrewd observation elicited a smile from the young man in spite of his abstraction.

"This difference," he replied, seriously, "is something; but it was not that which decided me in my opinion. If greater or less perfection of the extremities regulated social distinctions, many mistresses would be servants. What struck me was this:

"When the two women rushed wildly from Mother Chupin's house, the woman with the small feet sprang across the garden with one bound, she darted on some distance in advance of the other. The horror of the situation, the vileness of the den, the horror of the scandal, the thought of a place of safety, inspired her with marvellous energy.

"But her strength, as often happens with delicate and nervous women, lasted only a few seconds. She was not half way from here to the Poivrière when her speed relaxed, her limbs trembled. Ten steps farther on she tottered and almost fell. Some steps farther, and she became so exhausted that she let go her hold upon her skirts; they trailed upon the snow, tracing a faint circle there.

"Then the woman with the broad foot came to her aid. She seized her companion around the waist; she dragged her along; their footprints here are mingled confusedly; then seeing that her friend was about to fall, she caught her up in her strong arms and carried her—and the footprints made by the woman with the small feet cease."

Was Lecoq merely amusing himself by inventing this story? Was this scene anything but a work of the imagination?

Was this accent of deep and sincere conviction which he imparted to his words only feigned?

Father Absinthe was still in doubt, but he thought of a way in which he might satisfy his uncertainty.

He caught up the lantern and hurried off to examine these footprints which he had not known how to read, which had been speechless to him, but which had yielded their secret to another.

He was obliged to agree with his companion. All that Lecoq had described was written there; he saw the confused footprints, the circle made by the sweeping skirts, the cessation of the tiny imprints.

On his return, his countenance betrayed a respectful and astonished admiration, and it was with a shade of embarrassment that he said:

"You can scarcely blame an old man for being a little like St. Thomas. I have touched it with my fingers, and now I am content to follow you."

The young policeman could not, indeed, blame his colleague for his incredulity.

"Then," Lecoq continued, "the accomplice, who had heard the fugitives coming, ran to meet them, and he aided the woman with the large feet in carrying her companion. The latter must have been really ill, for the accomplice took off his hat and used it in brushing the snow from this plank. Then, thinking the surface was not yet dry enough, he wiped it with the skirt of his overcoat. Were these civilities pure gallantry, or the usual attentions of an inferior? I have asked myself that question.

"This much, however, is certain: while the woman with the small feet was recovering her strength, half reclining upon this board, the other took the accomplice a little to one side, five or six steps away to the left, just by that enormous block of granite.

"There she talked with him, and, as he listened, the man leaned upon the snow-covered stone. His hand left a very distinct imprint there. Then, as the conversation continued, he rested his elbow upon the snowy surface."

Like all men of limited intelligence, Father Absinthe had suddenly passed from unreasoning distrust to unquestioning confidence.

Henceforth he would believe anything, from the same reason that had, at first, made him believe nothing.

With no idea of the bounds of human reasoning and penetration, he saw no limits to the conjectural genius of his companion.

With perfect faith, therefore, he inquired:

"And what was the accomplice saying to the woman with the broad shoes?"

If Lecoq smiled at his naïveté, the other did not suspect it.

"It is rather difficult for me to answer that question," he replied. "I think, however, that the woman was explaining to the man the immensity and imminence of the danger that threatened his companion, and that they were trying to devise some means to rescue him from it. Perhaps she brought him orders given by the murderer. It is certain that she ended by beseeching the accomplice to run to the Poivriére and see what was passing there. And he did so, for his tracks start from this block of granite."

"And only to think," exclaimed the officer, "that we were in the hovel at that very moment. A word from Gevrol, and we might have had handcuffs on the whole gang! How unfortunate!"

Lecoq was not sufficiently disinterested to share his companion's regret.

On the contrary, he gave heartfelt thanks for Gevrol's blunder. Had it not been for that, how would he ever have found an opportunity of interesting himself in an affair that grew more and more mysterious, but which he hoped to fathom finally?

"To conclude," he resumed, "the accomplice soon returned, he had witnessed the scene, he was afraid, and he hastened back. He feared that the thought of exploring the premises might enter the minds of the police. It was to the lady with small feet that he addressed himself. He explained the necessity of flight, and told her that even a moment's delay might be fatal. At his words, she summoned all her energy; she rose, and hastened, clinging to the arm of her companion.

"Did the man indicate the route they were to take, or did they know it themselves? This much is certain; he accompanied them some distance, in order to watch over them.

"But above the duty of protecting these women, he had a still more sacred duty to perform—that of succoring his accomplice, if possible. He retraced his steps, passed her again, and the last footprint that I can discover leads in the direction of the Rue du Château-des-Rentiers. He wished to know what would become of the murderer, and went to place himself in his path."

Like a dilettante who can scarcely restrain his applause until the close of the *morceau* that delights him, Father Absinthe had been unable to repress his admiration entirely.

But it was not until Lecoq ceased speaking that he gave full vent to his enthusiasm.

"Here is a detective!" he exclaimed. "And they say that Gevrol is shrewd! What has he ever done to compare with this? Ah! shall I tell you what I think? Very well. In comparison with you, the general is only John the Baptist."

Certainly the flattery was gross, but it was impossible to doubt its sincerity. This was the first time that the balmy dew of praise had fallen upon Lecoq's vanity; it delighted him.

"Nonsense," he replied, modestly; "you are too kind, papa. After all, what have I done that is so very clever? I told you that the man was of middle age. It was not difficult to see that after one had examined his heavy and rather dragging step. I told you that he was tall—an easy matter. When I saw that he had been leaning upon that block of granite there to the left, I measured the aforesaid block. It was sixty-seven inches in height, consequently a man who could rest his elbow upon it must be at least six feet high. The impress of his hand proves that I am not mistaken. On seeing that he had brushed away the snow which covered the plank, I asked myself what he had used; I thought that it might be his cap, and the mark left by the visor proves that I was right.

"Finally, if I have discovered the color and the material of his overcoat, it is only because when he wiped off the wet board, some splinters of the wood tore off a few tiny flakes of brown wool, which I found, and which will figure in the trial. But what does this amount to, after all? Nothing. We have discovered only the first elements of the affair. We hold the clew, however; we will follow it to the end. Onward, then!"

The old officer was electrified, and, like an echo, he repeated: "Forward!"